BECOMING

from chaos to alignment through
allowance, flow, and belief

by Tracie Bork

Book design by April Bell
Cover image adapted from photo by Rainhard Wiesinger

ISBN: 979-8-9916712-0-0

To protect the privacy of certain individuals, the names, identifying details, and some locations have been changed.

*This book is dedicated to my partner, Adam,
for loving me unconditionally, believing in me, and
supporting me, always.*

Introduction

Growing up, I believed the way to succeed at life was to control situations, plan in excruciating detail, and exert my incredibly powerful will. I thought I knew just how my life would unfold. Unfortunately, life had other plans.

In this book, I tell the story of my life as a scientist who achieved great career heights while reeling from early trauma. It chronicles the complex way my body broke down and the hope, reassurance, and peace I found in the unexpected and the unknown. This is ultimately a memoir of spiritual awakening; the strength and answers I received in the knowing that miracles are available to everyone and every moment a blessing to be cherished.

I wrote this book to honor my soul and its journey and for The Divine who patiently waited for me. I wrote this book to inspire others to listen to the inner voice they may not acknowledge and still others to trust in their own intuition. We need the discernment to listen to our inner voice and follow it wherever it may lead us. It may take us on a very unexpected journey, but those unfamiliar paths may benefit us the most. Our prospects and opportunities are endless when we remain open to new and different possibilities or thoughts.

PART ONE

The Long Way Home

CHAPTER 1

The Emergency Room, Boulder, Colorado

I was hit with a painful condition called trigeminal neuralgia. It's a type of chronic pain that affects a nerve in your face and jaws. I distinctly remember that it was not what I told Santa I wanted for Christmas, but he was a shmuck that year, and that's what I received.

At first, the pain came and went in cycles; twenty minutes of pain followed by twenty minutes of relief. I thought I could handle it, but then the pain stopped cycling. Both the lower and upper jaws on the right side hurt like I was getting root canals without any anesthesia. I had no idea what brought it on, and frankly, I just wanted it to stop.

I thought I knew what pain was; but I must have been delusional. I've had migraines that left me devastated and immobile for nine days. Those migraines were nothing compared to this all-consuming pain. When medical professionals describe trigeminal neuralgia as among the most painful conditions known to mankind, they mean it. I was ready to kill myself.

It was Christmas Eve. My neurologist was off-duty hopefully enjoying the holidays. The on-call neurologist required blood work before he prescribed anything. My partner, Adam, and I headed to the hospital.

The prescription I was given had a long list of warnings, so I didn't want anything to do with it. Adam was persuasive. He repeatedly asked how long I was going to writhe around before taking it. Eventually, I gave in.

The medication stopped the pain, but I saw space portals in our backyard. I was wide awake but hallucinating. This was fine since I wasn't alone, but it would have been terrifying otherwise. Looking back, I can confirm that these were indeed hallucinations. This wasn't anything about perceiving energy. This was years before I was thinking about such things.

I was able to see my neurologist several days later (it was Christmas, after all). I was figuring space portals meant my dose was quite high enough, and my neurologist agreed and promptly labelled me a lightweight. I switched to a much lower dose. I was bisecting a children's chewable tab. Adam and I quickly nicknamed them BAM-BAMs since no two pharmacies could manage to tell us how to phonetically pronounce it the same way. We preferred the unlikely, but amusing, car-BAM-aze-pine. Just try saying that while keeping a straight face.

I read the handout and was immediately concerned about the rare rashes they mentioned. My body tends to excel at the rare and unlikely side effects. I tried to forget I ever read that. When I started getting a slight itch on my scalp, I was hoping for dandruff or eczema—I've been known to get eczema when stressed. If I ever deserved to be stressed, it would be now. I had Adam start taking pictures. The images didn't match anything I was seeing in the literature, so I remained unworried—for the most part. My belief at this time was that my knowledge alone could get me out of this situation and keep me safe. If I understood everything, everything would be okay.

Fast forward a few months to March 12, 2013. We awoke to unexpected snow. I ate my BAM-BAM, a slice of apple, started drinking my cup of coffee, and I began feeling very flushed and hot. I went to the bathroom to check my reflection and calmly told Adam, "We need to get to the hospital right now." I was having a full-blown allergic reaction.

I didn't have trouble breathing yet, but I knew it could come at any point. I was bright red in a full-face flush with hives on my chest. I went to my purse get an EpiPen and my albuterol inhaler. We got out to the car and to the main thoroughfare only to discover the unexpected snow meant travel was impossible. Traffic was backed up in all directions. Fortunately, we're only a short distance from a big fire station, and I, most relieved, pointed Adam in that direction. Paramedics.

The fire station staff acted quickly, inserted an IV line, monitoring my breathing to ensure my airway was not shutting down, and called an ambulance. We arrived at the hospital, and discovered the emergency room doctor was someone we'd seen several times before. I felt more secure in seeing someone I'd dealt with previously. They stabilized me, and then we all tried to figure out what set me off. I'd been taking BAM-BAMs for several months, so nobody ever even considered that. The only other thing I had consumed was the apple slice. We all concurred that it must have been something on the apple. I am allergic to a lot of different food items; why not apples now? I showed him the scalp rash and asked if it could be the BAM-BAMs. He said no with great confidence.

The doctor made me promise to never hesitate about using an EpiPen again. Yeah, yeah, I know. Allergic reactions can ramp up faster than you can control them, and once past a certain point, you're screwed (so to speak).

So there we had it: a diagnosis of an apple allergy. There's lots of foods I can't eat anymore; what's one more thing? On we went with our lives.

Insert scary music here.

It was time to pack for our trip to Japan, a country Adam and I both love and had visited many times. Before the trip, I sent photos of my rash, which at this point was keeping me awake and driving me nuts, to both my functional medicine physician, Dr. Jill, and my neurologist. I didn't hear anything. We check email when we are away, so I figured I'd hear from them if it were anything important.

 I'm constantly amazed how we continue to think that email communication is always immediate; it just simply doesn't work in that fashion. Instead of hours, sometimes it takes days because it was delayed for some silly server reason. So it was in this case.

I always have an EpiPen with me, but I brought six with us on vacation. I remember staring at them and thinking odd things about my mental state. If you need more than two EpiPens and aren't near a hospital for additional help, you probably aren't going to make it. What's the use in bringing six? I figured it was harming no one so ignored my inner voice of reason.

CHAPTER 2

Japan, Part 1

On March 24 we left for Japan, starting our trip in Tokyo before heading to Kobe. On March 28, after eating my evening BAM-BAM, I had another allergic reaction. Obviously, we now knew that the culprit was the BAM-BAM and not apples. This reaction wasn't as bad as the last one at home, but I still needed to get to an emergency room.

We went to Tokyo University Hospital where we met Dr. Gunshin. He spoke perfect English which was very nice since our Japanese is limited to very simple phrases and words. He and two of his students examined me. I was not in danger of expiring, but they gave me drugs to calm my immune system for the evening and more for the following morning. I had been out in the sun that day when we went out to Odaiba to see the big Gundam, so he thought it was more a sun reaction. This is common in people who are taking BAM-BAMs.

The next morning, we excitedly hopped onto a shinkansen (bullet train) to head to Kobe. I had the paperwork from Dr. Gunshin and the ER visit tucked into my purse. I took my morning BAM-BAM with no ill effect; this was understandable given I also took another whopping dose of the drug Dr. Gunshin had prescribed which would compensate for any allergic reaction I had.

However, when I took the evening dose, it elicited a very different response. My cheeks turned bright red, my breathing changed noticeably, and my skin begin to feel like something was crawling underneath it. I knew we had to get to a hospital right now, yet again.

The hotel got us into a cab. We were quickly on our way, but my breathing was becoming progressively and dangerously shallower. I asked the driver how long to the hospital. He depressed the accelerator and replied five minutes. I had an EpiPen out, but the cab was now careening about, Adam and I bouncing against each other in the back seat. With all this motion, we couldn't accurately inject the epinephrine. The vehicle was moving too fast for me to use the EpiPen and yet possibly too slow to save my life.

The odd things I was thinking about my mental state when I packed the EpiPen I was now holding in my hand came back in a flash. I brought six but can't even accurately administer one injection. Thoughts of death, once abstract, were now very real and imminent. Was this the end?

And how did I get here?

CHAPTER 3

California

I was only three years old when my father went to war in 1965. I've thought about it quite a lot over my lifetime, and I can easily say it is the single most influential thing that ever happened to me. I remember making cookies with my mother to box up and send to him. "Are these cookies going to Daddy?" I would ask. "Yes," my mother would say. I would then inquire as to why I couldn't be boxed up with the cookies so that I could go visit him.

My mother had a habit of inadvertently waking me up at night with her activities. In fairness, I can't imagine how distraught she must have been with thoughts of possibly becoming a widow with three small children under six years old. I would hear noise in the middle of the night, and thinking my father had returned I would get up to investigate. It was only my mother repeatedly ironing his uniforms to keep herself busy. I didn't understand this as a child and would inwardly fume. Even into my adulthood, noise that woke me provoked an oddly aggressive response. It wasn't just my sleep being interrupted. It was that patterning, like a worn groove in a record, replaying over and over.

My father is 100% the military man. I grew up with strict discipline and the 7 P's: Proper Previous Planning Prevents Piss Poor Performance. It was drilled into me continuously. Achieve. Behave. Conform. Perform. No wonder I turned out to be such an over-achiever and people-pleaser. It may have helped me academically, but it took a toll on my body.

My parents eloped to get married. My father's mother was adamantly against the marriage, and my mother was tired of waiting for approval that would never come. She stopped saying "no" and became pregnant. Her mother, Marion, was a schoolteacher who suffered with migraines and, hence, addiction to painkillers. Her father was a brilliant engineer who fought in WWII. Upon his return to civilian life, the demons of war tormented him endlessly, and he became an alcoholic. He eventually stopped drinking through sheer will and the Bible. I remember them both so fondly. My grandmother crawling around the floor chasing us while hiding under her mink and looking like a ferocious bear. My grandfather, Leo, smacking us on the butts with his newspaper as we ran through the house and played.

My father's parents were different. His father Ernest's family escaped the Alsace-Lorraine region and the terror which was Europe before 1917. They arrived in the US, and Ernest's father, Gustuv, changed their last name from Borkkowski to Bork to not appear so conspicuously German. Ernest worked under his father as a blacksmith repairing logging equipment for the booming logging industry but left because Gustuv kept his pay. Ernest found work at other jobs and as a moonshiner. He eventually married Geraldine who worked at a convent. Her God was punishing, judgmental, and unforgiving. Everyone felt her wrath. Where he was gentle and sweet, she was manipulative, plotting, and sharp-tongued. I still remember him jovially yelling at her, "F- the Pope!" when she tried his patience. Their family was very large and times were tough. They lived on an orchard in Hood River, where my father had great childhood adventures. He and his many brothers ran like animals with little to no discipline (my father's words).

Because my dad was in the military, we were always stationed elsewhere and rarely saw relatives of any kind. I believe my parents liked it that way; they felt they had escaped their past. They were wrong, of course, but the field of epigenetics (how your behavior and environment can affect how your genes are read and work) didn't exist at that time.

Most of my earliest memories are of naval hospitals and various medical facilities. My mother would say that I was sick from the day I was born, but that in itself tells you something. I was prone to chest infections. I had my tonsils removed. I had seemingly endless allergies to various medications and food. Later in life, I learned a wealth of information which would explain my allergies, food sensitivities, and much more. But I still don't know to this day if I was sick because everyone kept telling me I was or because there was something actually wrong every single time I went. I'm sure it was a combination of the two, but the takeaway for me was that I was broken, unwell, and could never hope for improvement.

My mother loved medical facilities. She loved reveling in her issues, discussing them endlessly, gaining sympathy from her listeners, and identifying with all of this. She loved retelling her stories of dealing with my strange myriad of illnesses which made for competitive conversations with other mothers about who was the biggest martyr—my child is sicker than yours and I have suffered the most. I somehow was part of that equation because I believe she additionally used me unconsciously to go there for a visit in the first place. "My daughter's so sick, but could you refill my prescription while we're here?"

She, like her mother before her, was afflicted with migraines. The doctor she first saw gave her a bottle of codeine and told her to take it until the pain stopped. That's how her addiction started. We now know that narcotics do little to nil for such pain, but the path had been laid. The addiction issues her parents had were passed down. Between her father's favorite mottos "pull yourself up by your bootstraps" and "just get it done (no complaining)", and her belief that anyone in the white coat of a doctor was a god, she had no room for doubt.

When my father returned from Vietnam, he came home a different person. Who wouldn't? We were not allowed to make igloos from sugar cubes for class projects; food waste or playing with food were tantamount to mortal sins. He angered easily, and we just tried to stay out of his way. Further into his military career, he was commanding hundreds of enlisted men on ships and doing what he would rather do—away from his family. I always felt that he enjoyed being at sea more than being home. Coming home from a long tour on the ship, my two older brothers and I wouldn't recognize him. Bearded from long months at sea, he would quickly become upset when we made noise or moved too fast. We were not the stoic crew who behaved as he thought we should. We quickly fell into line because we feared him, but it typically took him yelling at us for us to realize we'd better revert to our military upbringing and stop acting like the children that we were.

As an adult, I recall finally finding the nerve to ask him what he was feeling back in 1965. I was imagining he must have been frightened to go to war, sad that he had to leave his young wife and three kids, fear he might die in a foreign land fighting a political war. I never expected to hear him say he was excited and intrigued about going on this journey of "going to war". I felt betrayed.

CHAPTER 4

Montana

When we moved from several tours in southern California (San Diego and Long Beach) to Montana, my father remained home except for the road travel which was required of him.

My father finished the inside of a van for our road trip moving from California to Montana. It became our home on the road, and us kids marveled at all the places we stopped to visit along the way. We kept our cat, Cricket, in a cage when needed, but she otherwise roamed the inside of the van. It was all so different than southern California. When we arrived in Helena, we set up in a KOA campground so we'd have access to shower facilities while we searched for a home.

My mother's health took a turn for the worse, and she had her first gallbladder attack. I remember speeding to the hospital with the flashing lights of an ambulance behind us. She was in the hospital for some time, and my father cared for us. We often visited her cousin's place to bathe as my father couldn't safely care for me alone at a campground where he couldn't enter the female facilities. I'd sit in the tub as he tried to wash and comb my hair. I know it was terribly difficult, those snarls and tangles in my long hair, and I never complained.

He seemed to like Montana because there was lots of fishing and hunting activities, all of which he was terribly skilled at from his childhood. He was quick to anger, however, and I thought it was his work setting and us kids' presence which was the biggest detriment to his happiness. We were just kids, and I think he couldn't control us the way he could his military underlings. That control was a specter in my life. The result was that I felt I needed to control everything, too, and that by doing so everything would work out the way I wanted.

Once we settled into Helena, I found a home in my biology class and particularly enjoyed the various anatomical models with the removable pieces so you could see how everything fit together and what was connected to what. I also enjoyed going to the rodeos and 4-H exhibits to visit all the animals. Ted, my oldest brother, was the excellent student he always was while Frank, the second oldest, continued to embarrass my father by stealing cigarettes from the local 7-11 so that my father was called from work to come to the police station and retrieve his son. Appearing at the police station still in uniform from work to discuss the illegal behavior of his son was not appreciated. Frank was finding attention in the only way he saw available to him, and he was punished for his efforts.

My father is an expert marksman, has the awards to prove his prowess, and delighted in teaching my two brothers and me how to shoot both pistols and rifles, and how to hunt and fish. I do remember lots of family moments huddling next to a fire while fishing on the Missouri River or up at Park Lake. Wandering through the woods he would patiently explain the need for hunting to cull the wildlife after coming across piles of bones of deer who starved during a particularly harsh winter. He has a wicked sense of humor, and I remember him telling me that deer backstroked across rivers to hide their antlers from view when I inquired how deer crossed rivers safely. He finished the unfinished basement in our home, and I remember marveling at how he could know how to do so many things like drywall, plumbing, masonry, and more.

I wanted more than anything to be like him. I wanted to seemingly know how to do everything, know the answer to all that is. I idolized my father, and in some sense, I guess I always will. The dangerous part for me is that I wanted to be like him because I thought somehow that would keep him from leaving again, that it would make him love me so much he wouldn't go away, that it would make him happy enough to stay home. I blamed myself for him preferring to be away from us. Some part of me was always the girl who wanted to be shipped in a parcel with the cookies so I could be with him.

CHAPTER 5

Alaska

The next tour was in Kodiak, Alaska, and my father was practically never home. We lived on the military base where the ships were, and the town of Kodiak was nine miles of paved road away. Ted and Frank rode a bus to town for school while I walked to school on base.

My mother had constant health issues, and since my father was at sea, it fell to me to cook and take care of things. I learned about drugs like Stelazine, Thorazine, and other anti-psychotics. I was eleven years old.

I remember the can on the kitchen counter with money for necessities, but I honestly have trouble remembering shopping at the base commissary for food. I would make things for my mother, pack it up in Tupperware and bring it to the dispensary where I visited her when she was ill. When she was home, she wasn't always in her right mind. Occasionally she would have seizures, and I would panic and run upstairs to our neighbor, Dr. Espisito, who was a dentist on the base. I remember standing in the bathroom and staring at my reflection in the mirror saying, "You have to be better than this. You have to do better than this." My heart still aches for that child who believed all that was happening was under her control, but the modeling my father had shown me was working. I truly believed if I could control everything, things would improve. My lack of control, I felt, was the reason for the craziness in my life. It was my fault.

Neighbors would bring us food which we occasionally accepted, but mostly my brothers and I refused outside help. We were just fine. Right? We didn't need anybody's help, and we certainly didn't want anybody's pity. We didn't need them. We were fine on our own. I ache when I think of refusing those homemade casseroles made by our neighbors who knew my father was at sea with their husbands, noticed my mother's absence, and were just trying to lighten our burdens.

I became fascinated with visiting the dispensary and talking with the various workers about what was wrong with my mother. I had my own share of viral infections and bronchitis, but it paled in comparison to what my mother was going through. She seemed to be a medical mystery to everyone. I loved watching the workers peer through microscopes telling me what they saw. I so wanted the answers so that I could know how to fix it and tell my father that I knew the answers, too. I am eternally grateful to the corpsmen in the lab who always humored me. They treated me with respect, answered my questions, and explained things even though I was probably a bother. I wish they could have known that they were feeding and caring for a budding scientist.

My school days were mixed. I loved my biology class with Mr. Fish who had chinchillas, snakes, rabbits, piranhas, and other creatures in his classroom. He gave me extra responsibilities of feeding some of the animals. I enjoyed math tremendously, but the teachers didn't have much to offer. Now I realize that the curricula for elementary school was unsuitable, and I would have had to take classes in town, off the base, for me to be challenged. It would have been difficult to send someone so young to be bussed into town for school. At first, they had me tutoring other students which further alienated me from my classmates. Flummoxed, the teachers then decided we would play different card games, and I became their fourth player in bridge. I never felt that I fit in with others my age. It was like we spoke different languages.

My father's departures were almost always spur of the moment and unannounced. This was his job as a military officer, to help people in the Gulf of Alaska who were in need; to us it just meant he was never around. The ships were docked adjacent to some of the activity centers and the exchange. Sometimes we'd go in with my father's ship present only to come out and find it missing. Everyone just understood he was gone again. Nobody said anything.

My brothers and I had no discipline when my father was gone, and my mother was constantly "missing". We were in heaven.

The base was outfitted with an extraordinary number of activities designed to help you (probably more for the adults) from going crazy given the remoteness of the station. You could paint, make pottery, watch movies in the cinema, bowl, and engage in any number of other indoor activities. My brothers and I made full use of all the organized activities and made up lots of others from items we looted, found, or made. We discovered all sorts of old military supplies including ammo, K-rations, tents and other survival gear in the numerous bunkers we located which were left over from World War II. We set up these scavenged tents in restricted areas just to see if we could get away with it, ran across the airplane runways right behind our house to test the response of base security, stole countless holiday decorations for the sheer thrill of it all, sledded off cliffs on sleds and in cardboard boxes, made snow forts and ones from actual timber high in the trees accessed by ladders, bought cans of beer from the Bachelor's Quarters vending machines, climbed Barometer Mountain at the end of the public airplane runway and Old Woman Mountain to swim in the lake on top in the summer, fished for Dolley Vardon off the Buskin Bridge, made stockpiles of snowballs which turned to ice balls for future fights, chased rabbits around the base with our pack of friends, swam in the ocean off Jewel Beach where the sand was mixed with endless smoothed colored glass from shipwrecks, and ran to spots we were told to avoid because of Kodiak bear incursions in order to watch the bears catch fish.

I imagine we acted a lot like my father and his many brothers in those days, running around the hills of Hood River. My older brothers, Ted and Frank, were both very protective of me. This was about to change dramatically.

Both of my parents were brought up in a strict Catholic manner. There was no other kind of Catholicism when they were young. When I was younger, my parents made sure we went to church. We memorized prayers, commandments, and my brothers went through confirmation.

My doubts first started when we first arrived in Helena, and we were living in a van in a KOA campground as we looked for a home. We always went to church, but the priest pulled my father aside to tell him we were dressed inappropriately (that is, not fancy enough). Even as a child I questioned what kind of church judged people for the way they dressed? It didn't seem right to me. In Kodiak we were enrolled in Catechism, and I immediately had problems. At first, I got kicked out because I asked too many questions. "If matrimony is one of the seven sacraments, what happens when people don't get married? I don't want to marry." This happened repeatedly. I knew I wasn't welcome, so I found a fire escape at the window in the back of the room to ditch class because I found it so unbelievable.

Frank became an altar boy and drank all the Communion wine with his friends. I found this poetic when, as an adult, I found out my father, too, was an altar boy. I wondered if he also drank the Communion wine with his friends.

During this time in Alaska my relationship with faith, which most people think of as organized religion or church services, quickly became incomprehensible. The final straw was a weekend when my father was actually home, and it was time for the weekly church visit and confession. He told me, smiling, that he hadn't done anything that week that required confession, so he wasn't going. I had an "a-ha" moment. How seriously were we taking this so-called faith or religion thing? I already didn't believe what they were telling me in Catechism and now my father says the "rules" don't apply to him? These collective experiences made me doubtful of anything to do with organized religion. Whatever it was religion was selling, I was no longer buying it.

CHAPTER 6

Pacific Northwest, Grandma's House

My father's ship was due in the yards in Seattle, Washington for normal repairs. It was decided we, too, would move stateside to live with my grandmother Marion and go to school while he was in Seattle working. We lived in different states, and I don't remember seeing my father during this time period. It was a ruse to get my mother out of Kodiak for a bit.

We were enrolled in school and told to lie. It was clear the schools weren't going to enroll us for just three months. I don't know how my brothers fared, but I was miserable. I didn't feel I could make friends or join the theater group or any other group because it was all just temporary. I don't remember a lot about school except I was unhappy, and the ordeal just served to cement my role as the imposter. My grandmother had changed from the person I used to know to this person who sat in bed in her clothes drinking coffee all day with her dresser top covered with prescription bottles. Leo, my grandfather, died when we first arrived in Kodiak, so I am sure that was part of the change. I remember my grandmother, my mother, and her sister, Marlene, all standing and looking at the numerous pill bottles and trading pills back and forth. It seems they were on a lot of the same scheduled drugs, so they would trade to cover each other while someone else's prescription was being refilled. I knew it meant trouble, and I was finally beginning to understand at some level why my father had such issues with my mother's family.

While Ted still protected me, Frank became belligerent and just plain scary. He frightened me. He had discovered cigarettes in the K-rations and marijuana while we were in Kodiak. He wasn't a very good student; he spoke through violence and once broke a boy's arm just for paying attention to me at a dance. Ted's stature made the coaches swoon with thoughts of their sports programs, but Ted, on the other hand, always favored history, speech debates, and socializing with his numerous friends.

After our three-month stint at my Grandmother Marion's ended when my father's ship repairs were finished in Seattle, we all returned to Kodiak to finish out my father's tour of duty.

I always thought that being a military kid was a superpower. You could adapt to anything, live anywhere, and you would survive. I believed constant goodbyes with friends were an inevitable part of our lives. But eventually, I realized this was a farce. My father was an officer and had powerful friends, so he got to choose where he wished to go next. There was always a family conversation supposedly discussing the options and where we preferred. I now realize it was my parents' feeble attempt at giving us a voice in the decision already made. We were off to Air Station North Bend, Oregon.

CHAPTER 7

Oregon, Part 1

School wasn't so bad at first. I was moved up in math and science, so I was able to go on the field trips to OMSI (Oregon Museum of Science and Industry) in Portland. I stayed awake all night watching the Foucault pendulum. I was such a geek. I made quick friends with an Army brat who seemed to be the other outcast of the eighth-grade class. North Bend is so small, people tend to stay put. Everyone has always known everyone else which makes military kids feel like imposters. We were unwelcome unknowns.

I began to be bullied and ostracized in school. I was smart, female, and small for my age. My parents hadn't allowed me to be moved up a grade because of my size; they only allowed advancement in certain classes like the sciences, math, and literature. I was constantly compared to Ted and Frank. "Bork, hmm, what kind of student are you?" they'd ask. Ted was Senior Class

President and on the debate team. He had friends of all strata. Frank found the outcasts, skipped school regularly, was always fighting, and was a prolific smoker of cigarettes. He was always in trouble, but those in control knew my father. When Frank ended up in jail, they'd call my dad to ask what to do with him. My father always retrieved him. My father eventually had to sign a contract with Frank and the school principal to ensure Frank's graduation—ironic given my father was the only one of his eight brothers to graduate. Ted and I were clearly held to a different standard. This never sat right with us.

By the time I was in high school the bullying increased. I excelled at chemistry and biology and even fermented strawberry wine at home for my biology project. One girl seemed to really despise me. I have no idea what prompted this. It became so bad that I stole some butyric acid, a colorless liquid fatty acid, from the chemistry lab. It only takes a little. Humans can pick this stuff up at 10 parts per million; it's the smell of vomit. I remember I was so distraught with the situation that I painted her locker with it and injected it through the vents at the top of the metal door in hopes of embarrassing her, giving her something else to be concerned about—a Revenge of the Nerds kind of scenario. Kids began to bully her because her locker gave off a horrendous odor. She never bothered me again.

I fell into the Future Business Leaders of America (FBLA) crowd because I took courses in Gregg shorthand and typing. Apparently I had a knack for it because the teacher asked me to travel around with the club to compete. I did and won many awards in both endeavors. I didn't mind doing it because it was a way to travel around the state and see new things. I was never stressed about it because the outcome didn't matter to me. I was attaining the skills I knew would be useful in college. If I was able to win some accolades for the school in the process, that was fine with me.

At this time, the economy was being gutted as the timber industry ground to a halt and jobs dried up. The spotted owl lived in old growth forests which were quickly being cut. When the bird became federally protected, the outcome was clear.

In response, to their credit, the high school instituted a curriculum where junior-year students picked a vocation to study like health care or mechanics. In junior year, students would learn all about their chosen vocation, and in senior year they would be placed in community programs where they could practice their skills. I was ecstatic. I chose health care, and I submerged myself in anatomy, bones, bodily systems, and physiology. I learned about decubitus ulcers, sucking chest wounds, foot drop, properly making beds, and much more. The skeleton in the class was my friend. I examined him closely discovering his secrets. This program would play a pivotal role in my life trajectory for years to come.

My mother had two major surgeries, and I once again became responsible for many things at home. I quit taking violin lessons which I had been taking since living in Montana. Cooking and household chores came first. I remember feeling cheated. Once I turned sixteen, I began to work as a waitress at a local franchise within walking distance. I found the work easy and used the time to allow my mind to wander. I'd recite cranial nerves and bones to myself while serving steaks. I made a lot of money in tips which pleased me. I guess I equated that with acceptance of some sort. My customers often teased that I could read their minds when it came to dealing with them. I now wonder if in some way I was intuiting what people wanted or needed, and that's why my income from tips was so phenomenal.

Ted continued to try to protect me while Frank verbally and physically abused me. He threw knives at me down the stairwell as I ran from the house. He locked me out when my parents were away. I've never understood why siblings won't tell on each other. Is it some sort of strange loyalty? The signs of abuse were evident. We had a pool table and Frank would jab me so hard with the cue that it left perfect little circle bruises on my body. One day he threw me into the shower stall with such force that my mother, working outside, heard me hit the wall. When that happened, she actually kicked him out of the house. Finally. I felt immense relief.

We adopted our cat, Cricket, while in southern California, and she was getting up there in her years. I do not remember any specifics about her being seriously ill, but one weekend when my parents and I went somewhere she disappeared. I stood out in the driveway calling for her. My mother was beside herself. We were both really upset, but it was decided she just probably went off somewhere and transitioned.

Later as an adult, Ted shared with me that my father had Frank put her in a box, take her out somewhere, and shoot her. Ted couldn't hold the secret any longer, so he told me. I was aghast, but unsurprised. This is how my father both does and doesn't deal with things. He deems the cat needs to go, so he arranges it, and doesn't tell anyone. He can't deal with other people's grief, let alone his own, so he just keeps it to himself. While that may be quick and painless for the cat, the amount of trauma done to the person doing the killing or learning about it later is phenomenal. We all got his message: you're not allowed to grieve because it is messy and makes him uncomfortable. Duly noted.[1]

---

[1]Many decades later, a compassionate veterinarian was called to the house of my parents to assist in the transition of one of their remaining cats. I believe the event was pivotal for all involved. It is difficult to remember that at any given time, we can change how we behave. We have the power to change our course, our path, through changing how we approach any situation.

CHAPTER 8

Guam

Ted graduated with honors, and Frank graduated per his contract with my father and the school principal. I was sixteen years old and finishing my junior year. Oh, look, it's time to move again! I couldn't believe it. I begged my father to let me stay. My brothers could take care of me. Believe me when I say we've had discussions about this now, and I realize how utterly absurd the request was. My brothers weren't even responsible for themselves and their actions. They were young men of eighteen and nineteen with many interests aside from their sister and her welfare. Oh, but I did not want to go. There was rally, and drill team, and FBLA, and—most importantly—my future job in healthcare in the community! Did they even have schools in this place called Guam, a US territory? My protests fell on deaf ears; father would not change his mind.

The humid tropical air hit me like a wet washcloth when we

stepped off the plane from Hawaii to Guam. It felt like breathing water, the air was so thick. I hated it. We were to live in the main naval station, but our housing wasn't ready upon our arrival. We were booked into a local motel. The motel occasionally had non-poisonous rat snakes coiled on the fence, encircling the pool. They were rather shy but seemed to want to join me for a swim when I went out at night to take a dip. As quickly as I got in, I jumped back out and watched them swim in the pool, so fluid, graceful, and effortless. I liked them, but it felt kind of creepy to think about swimming with them. I think most of the people staying at the motel were military coming to or going from Guam. They remained closeted away in their rooms, or searched for air-conditioned relief at other places, so we rarely saw anyone else.

We went to classes to alert us to some of the dangers of living on Guam. For instance: don't snorkel or dive and collect pretty shells and then toss your bag over your shoulder. The Cone shell inhabitants have a deadly neurotoxin and will sting you through your shell bag, paralyzing you; use a clean beach bottle to collect shells instead. Don't ignore any cut or injury from a coral reef; seek quick medical attention. These can be difficult to heal and often require expert intervention. Some of the island's dangers were not appropriate to discuss in the classroom; however, these are where most of the danger lay.

Our per diem was all about the food. My father seemed to always find the best places to eat. He dealt with so many different people, and I am sure that food was always part of the discussion. What's your favorite place to eat? Whether it was the fancy restaurant with menus painted on old Lancer's wine bottles, the dimly lit intimate Japanese clubs, a local downtrodden place with dead flies in the windows, or the Chinese restaurant where we became such regulars that we didn't order from the menu, he delighted in bringing us to new places and trying new food. My father became a different person here, relaxed and approachable. We connected on the same things at the same level, having contests on who could pick up the smallest item with their chopsticks. Food became a way to connect, and this is where I felt closest to him.

The island was such a mix of cultures: the indigenous Chamorro people, Chinese, Japanese, Thai, Filipino, and all of us Coast Guard, Navy, and Air Force folks. The food was amazing, but the military did not mix well with the more relaxed cultures. I actually don't think the military mixes well with anyone. No judgement, just facts. I easily picked out military personnel at the more upscale restaurants, but I rarely saw any other of my kind at the more far-flung local places my father found for us to try out.

After more than a month of eating out constantly, and exploring the island through food, we moved into the fortress of the naval air station and into our typhoon-proof, cinderblock house on base. It was kind of like living in a bowling alley. You had to use shoe stands in the closet otherwise shoes molded to the floor, so there were, obviously, no carpets. Did I mention the cute gecko lizards which were everywhere and the flying roaches which seemed far too big to be actual insects? Unload your groceries outside—no cardboard or paper in the houses because it brings in baby roaches and eggs. The big ones would occasionally fly in when you opened the door, and they were large enough you could hear them skitter about the tile floor. Charming place.

I made sure my parents knew how unhappy I was to be there every single day. Of course, nothing was going to change; this was my father's new assignment, and we had to see it through. Eventually, as I had done before, I resigned myself to the situation and discovered more of this exotic place around me. The three of us soon made the most of it and spent time finding new locations to swim and search for beautiful shells while enjoying the amazing variety of foods available.

Every weekend we went to The Green Revolution, an open market serving every type of food you could want. Its name came from the market's beginning when they traded and sold plants after a typhoon stripped the island of vegetation. My father and I went crazy enjoying all they had to offer: eggrolls, red rice, grouper, gamson, barracuda, dolphinfish, snapper, skipjack, yellowfin, pancit, adobo, crispy duck, lumpia, tempura, finadenne, chicken kelaguen, hotnon babui, BBQ short ribs, sashimi, and sushi. My father and I typically went in different directions in the market leaving my mother to save a table. This gave me the opportunity to infuse myself with the colors of the arrays of offerings, the sounds of all the different languages, the smells of the enticing foods. The people at the market were exceptionally friendly and seemed to enjoy my obvious pleasure in the wide variety of their food. They would smile broadly at me, the energy of their smiles contagious, pointing and laughing at my ever-filling plate, making suggestions, teaching me new words and new foods and new accents. I salivated while making choices and filling my plate, wanting to try it all. We met back at my mother's location and compared plates, tasting what each of us had chosen to bring back to the table.

Due to my dad's position, we were invited to many weekend fiestas at local villages which made the Green Revolution's offerings look paltry. There was escabeche, snake, fiesta dog, fanihi, and endless desserts like latiya, bunelos aga or gollai appan lenmai.

My parents would spend their existence on Guam on the base behind the tall chain-link fences topped with concertina wire. I am quite sure they looked at the secure base as a fortress while I, at sixteen, looked at it as a prison. All the enticing things seemed to be off-base: bars, dance clubs, beaches, endless exotic food choices, and other young people. I wanted to experience and devour life, not just survive it. There was a literal smorgasbord of choices available, and I wanted to ingest it all.

I went to school and worked off the base. I found out that I was one of two blonde women on the island which is 314 square miles of mostly jungle. There were no military schools, and I planned to try to finish high school with the hopes of receiving my diploma from my high school in North Bend. Off to the high school we went for a meeting with the counselors. Several important things happened while we were there.

The first one alerted me to my station in the local society. I wore a dress. I followed my father up a flight of outside stairs. (It's too hot and humid to have hallways and inside alcoves and the like; everything that can be is open.) littered with local boys. As we went up the stairs, they tugged my dress and made suggestive rude sounds. I'd experienced this stateside so remained silent. When one boy pinched my calf, however, my step faltered, and I looked directly at him. His leer spoke of the clear intention behind that skin-on-skin contact. I felt it in his humid touch on my tropically-hot bare skin. I saw it in his eyes. I was in danger in this place. Quite literally, I needed to watch my every step. I was on my own here. My father either didn't notice or chose not to. I still don't know which.

The meeting with the school counselor was a huge win for me, though. They didn't have a high school vocational program like the one I had been enrolled in stateside, but the counselor knew the right people and would make it happen through the community college. The first person I would report to was Janice, who ran her own medical labs downtown at the ITC Building. Then I would work at a Seventh-day-Adventist-run urgent care clinic, followed by a stint with a coroner on the island. I couldn't believe my luck. I think my father would have agreed to anything I wanted at this point. He hadn't yet realized what this place was really like.

I had to drive off-base, as I mentioned, so I got a used Datsun pickup I used to toss my fins and swimming gear in for quick runs to the beach. The bed was covered with a coating to protect it from corroding and getting what was fondly called car cancer from the salt air, humidity, and heat. I started school, and my father started work.

He oversaw and was responsible for all sorts of men beneath his rank. He had daily intelligence which informed him of local bars and other locations NOT to let his people go because it was simply too dangerous. He saw the trouble his men got into at local venues because they were outsiders, and I know he was probably terrified for my safety. I believe this because of a conversation we once had where he told me, in no uncertain terms, never to get out of my car anywhere but on the base with the Marine sentries. If I had trouble, whether it be personal or a traffic issue, I was to drive back to base even if the police wanted me to stop. Never get out of the car. If the police took me into custody, he may never find me. Okay, Dad. Good to know. Little did he know what I was experiencing at school was simply unacceptable.

The kids I went to school with had never seen a woman of my coloring before. Blue eyes and blond just didn't occur in this habitat. I thought I would be lost in the crowd of students, but I was wrong. I stopped wearing dresses after the first day because mine was ripped from my body. I remember that dress clearly. I had sewn it myself. A below-the-knee dress of light yellow material with tiny raised fuzzy dots, it didn't last the first morning at school. The guys would tug fiercely at a sleeve until it detached from the shoulder; pulling at the skirt repeatedly as I walked between them cloth would disengage from the waist-band. The disarray of the dress only served to feed their ravenous behavior. I left campus early that day after making the dress sleeveless and wrapping the skirt material around my waist like a beach wrap. I wore jeans the next day. No, it was not pleasant but remember that I had been abused by Frank for years. Not this type of sexually-intimidating abuse, but physical abuse just the same whether it was being punched or hit or thrown into the shower stall. I would not be daunted. I just found a different way to approach the problem.

I was threatened with knives, so I began to carry a fixed-blade, unscabbarded, Gerber hunting knife in my purse so that I could stab it directly through the leather of my purse if need be. There was a security force on campus, but it was mostly to keep the various gangs in line by simply having a police-like presence on campus. They effectively did nothing except take bribes from different gangs to allow for smooth drug trafficking. It wasn't meant to help with personal issues; nobody did anything.

Not long after I started at the high school, I sat cross-legged on a bench studying, massive physics book open in my lap, when I noticed a white-clad figure in front of me. I could see his dark skin against the white clothing and noticed his crotch was fully visible, intensely dark against white cloth. I would not look. Would not meet his eyes. Would not validate his presence. I was sixteen, had never seen a penis before, and this was not going to be the first one. I didn't know whether I had time to get up and run, or if he would reach out and grab me. I had no experience with men in the throes of lust and orgasm. I pushed my heavy book down against my crotch further protecting me, shielding me. He masturbated on the sidewalk in front of me as I sat frozen. I so wished I could meld with the wall behind me. I was terrified, but I came up with a demeaning wisecrack as he finished to show him I wasn't afraid. Yeah, right. This is how I had learned to cope with the unacceptable. Make light of everything as if it were a joke. Downplay the seriousness of any situation. Pretend everything was normal in my horribly abnormal and dangerous world.

The high school campus was fenced, and you were only allowed to leave if you had a pass which you had to show at the gates. Yet another example of a fortress or a prison, but this was definitely a prison meant to keep the "students" on-campus and, supposedly, in class. With its myriads of gangs, drugs, crime, and security personnel who ignored their surroundings, it definitely operated as a prison. I went to school to take trigonometry, probability and statistics, and physics. The classes were filled with military kids stuck in the same boat as me. The classes were well-taught and engaging, and then we were thrown back into the wild of the general population. I walked through the crowds of boom boxes blaring Michael Jackson's "Don't Stop 'til You Get Enough" and The Knack's "My Sharona" to my truck, locked the doors, and left the windows rolled up even in the heat until I was away from campus. I left that craziness to return to what was truly my passion: my work.

I met an outgoing local girl, Lolin, and we became fast friends. The island is very Catholic; she was the youngest of twelve, if I recall correctly. She longed to get out of Guam. She loved to hear stories of the United States, and I was accepted into her group of female friends. Lolin taught me a decent vocabulary of her native language, and I learned a lot being constantly bombarded with it. I also picked up the inflections and accents which my father did not appreciate. We would go out to the clubs and dance all night. There was no legal drinking age enforced. I was pretty mindful of where my father told me NOT to go at first, but I soon realized there might also be young military men at these other places who were skirting their own orders. It was all just too attractive. I saw peep shows, strip clubs, and various attractions I am sure no sixteen-year-old should see.

Occasionally the clubs would be raided by the military police to retrieve their enlisted men. I would find a cupboard or closet behind the bar and hide until the danger had passed. I was willing to skirt the rules, but I would not embarrass my father. The Marine sentries at the base were my friends, and I made them cookies and snacks to cement that loyalty. I needed them not to alert my father of my comings and goings in the wee hours of the morning when I came home from the clubs, and I needed them to protect me should I ever need their help with the local law enforcement. While they saluted my father as we went through the gates, I knew they were secretly smiling because they'd just waved me through after an ID check hours before.

CHAPTER 9

The Labs

At Janice's lab, I learned parasitology and blood work. I made blood smears to do differentials (routine tests to count cell types), identified various parasites in the smears, and ran blood chemistry profiles. We had various machines like Coulter Blood Analyzers to help us, but the machinery was constantly breaking down and in need of service because they weren't meant to run at the ambient temperature and humidity of Guam. It would spit out paper with high values in red ink and normal in black. Most of the read outs were red given the poor health and dietary deficiencies of the island populace. I worked in concert with the other techs, but my work was always checked, and Janice kept a close watch. I was taught to respect samples and chemicals because of possible contagion or danger—not to fear my work.

I learned phlebotomy, how to draw blood. It was easy for me, but I had many difficult situations because patient dehydration, extra weight, or stubborn veins made it more challenging. I could draw myself, and we often used our own blood as controls or baselines as the test reagents were constantly going bad because of the heat. We kept charts of our own results to watch and compare as the new normal against our wealth of patients. One of the more senior technicians used a textbook with formulas to run all the blood chemistries by hand in test tubes when the machines went down for extended periods of time. I thought it was magical to watch her read the formulas, make additions to the many tubes, and watch for reactions like color change. I could see that it took great concentration as she made dilutions and additions with varied pipettes.

The Seventh-day Adventist urgent care clinic and laboratory was faster paced and very exciting. I wore a lab coat (it was so hot that I wore a tube top under a lab coat plus pants), and I could do anything. I was much more exposed to patients not just having their blood drawn, but bringing in random samples for the lab, drawing patients in the ER, and dealing with walk-ins for the emergency services. The woman who ran the bacteriology section of the lab soon had me making all the agar and agar plates for seeding, taught me which plates to use for which patient sample, how to apply antibiotic discs to plates and choose the appropriate drug, and schooled me about the various bacteria and how they appeared. From my earlier childhood, I had perfected the "nothing bothers me, there is nothing wrong" expression, so I impressed the adults on staff when I didn't run screaming from the room when faced with an emergency. Downplay the seriousness of any situation. Pretend everything was normal in my horribly abnormal and dangerous world.

It was here that I learned why the dairy from the island made me violently ill. When I was running bacteria counts on the milk samples, I saw that they were using coconut milk as a filler. It must be the coconut that I am highly allergic to, I surmised. No more dairy for me. I would end up running the VDRLs (screening test for syphilis) in batches after the diplomats traveled. Because of my parasitology knowledge from Janice's lab, I could screen stool smears for ova. I gained a strong dislike for worms, and it was amazing how many people had them. A woman with a baby on her hip came in and slid a crumbled paper towel over the counter. When I saw it had worms in it, I asked her where she got them. She pointed to her infant. Oh my.

When the technician who ran the bacteriology section of the lab went on vacation, she announced I was the most qualified to sit in for her. I figured that's what she had been planning all along since the other techs were scared or disgusted with the microbes and had no interest. I had no fear, just a healthy respect for all the different patient samples and for all the different microbes they contained. To me it was a mini experiment with every sample from every patient I dealt with. Sputum, stool, urine, or blood, all were handled differently and plated differently. Once I had a draw of a particularly ill patient. I made two blood cultures to put in the incubator. Blood cultures are notorious for possible contamination because they often must sit for long periods of time in the incubator. By the time something grows you think, "ah that's contamination," unless you have another that appears just like the twin culture. This patient had tuberculosis. I once drew another patient and made blood slides only to find Plasmodium—the patient had malaria. The director reported it and then handed the slides over to the CDC.

A construction worker came through the front doors one day dripping blood from his back. I sat him down and applied pressure to his back wound with clean dressing from a nearby cart until I could get the attention of someone else (without screaming, "Can't you see this man is bleeding?"). Somebody on staff noticed the blood on the floor about the same time a couple of his buddies ran in with tool belts clanging. They were from a nearby construction site: He had fallen and been poked by some reinforcement bar on the way down. He just walked away while they safely descended the building and followed his blood trail down the street. The injured man insisted on my presence in the ER as I seemed to be a calming influence for him—the first person he saw after his accident. This work gave me purpose; I was helping others. I never knew what would happen on any given day. While this might make for a fulfilling and exciting job, it also taught my threat response (limbic system) to always remain on high alert, watching and waiting for the next thing to happen, the other shoe to drop. Little did I know then that my high drive was accelerating more than a career, but also a medical condition I'd spend the rest of my life coming to terms with.

Limbic System Impairment

Our limbic system is the part of the brain involved in our behavioral and emotional responses we need for survival. It is commonly referred to as the part of your brain responsible for the fight, flight, or freeze response. A healthy system sees a threat, maybe a tiger, and plans to fight the tiger, freeze (hide), or run (flight). Once the tiger is dealt with in whichever manner was deemed most efficient, the brain goes back to a baseline, normal, safe state until excited again by an outside threat. At that time the limbic system kicks again to present the fight, flight, or freeze choices. We live best in that normal, baseline state.

I understand fully now that my life experiences and upbringing resulted in my limbic system getting stuck in the threat-response mode. I was constantly ready to fight and saw everything and everyone as a threat to be dealt with. I never returned to baseline and my nervous system was constantly on high alert, flooding my body with chemicals which were unhealthy for me. Simply put, I saw tigers everywhere. From the people I hung out with to the situations I attracted and found myself in, it was all set up perfectly for dysfunction. I take responsibility as I was gaining life force from adrenaline and drama, but that is over now. I've finished. I actual-

ly investigated this possibility of a limbic system issue
back in 2015, but somehow it didn't stick, the program
wasn't right, or it just wasn't my journey at that time.
It took seeing an article from a functional medicine
doctor I follow to bring it to my attention again. About
a year later, a friend brought it to my attention yet again.
Knowing there are no coincidences, this time I paid
attention and began investigating in earnest. There are a
handful of different approaches available to retrain your
limbic system and knock it out of its fight/flight/freeze
mode. Copious reviews agree that there are a handful
of methods from holistic to regimented that work. It's
all a personal choice for which fits best to the individual. These programs retrain your brain by realizing our
brains become addicted to chemicals like adrenaline and
need to be retrained to recall how to live a pleasant and
joyful life of experiencing dopamine, oxytocin, sero-
tonin, and endorphins (our happy chemicals). Yes, just
like any addiction, it takes time to change patterns and
brain responses to a healthy state. The longer your brain
has functioned in a maladapted state, a state of limbic
system malfunction, well, habits are hard to break. More
to the point, neuroplasticity takes time and repetition.
Expect a possible issue with your limbic system who has
been the 3-year-old in the driver seat for a long time.
It wants its dose of cortisol and adrenaline, and it will
resist changes.

I have seen marvelous online videos of a teacher of neuro-plasticity and movement which explain the theory of a threat bucket. He has a bucket of water and explains with each additional scoop of water added (stress to the nervous system), we approach the top until it is overflowing at which point the person begins to display neurological symptoms. Our job, he explains, is to continually find ways to take water back out of the bucket, lowering the water or threat level through exercise, movement, meditation, and many other proven techniques. I didn't see these videos until I was in my fifties, but they explain what was happening when I was seventeen.

When you are working in bacteriology, you use both hands and take great care not to set test tube tops or anything else down on surfaces to prevent contamination. You hold tools and agar plates up off the bench, using fingers to keep things balanced, pinky fingers to squeeze tops off tubes or replace caps. This is quite the dance. At first you will need to set down things, being exceedingly cautious to avoid contamination and continually wiping down your bench between samples. Once you get the hang of it, though, there is no need that anything touches the bench. It all remains suspended in your hands. Great finger dexterity helps. Imagine my surprise when, some time after mastering these techniques, the test tube tops just started dropping from my right baby finger. I seemed to have no strength in the nerve needed to hold that position (the ulnar nerve). I also noticed that flexion of my neck produced pins and needles sensations in my feet.

My father set up an appointment with a neurologist who decided it was my stress response and excitation around the thought of going back to the United States on my own and starting college. I think his diagnosis was polite, but that it was actually signals from my nervous system that my threat bucket was already overflowing. I didn't want to admit it, but the amount of stress I was under, combined with the anxiety from my childhood, was causing physical symptoms in my body.

CHAPTER 10

Fight, Flight, Freeze

I met Randy at the base rec pool. Randy, part Tahitian, had the most amazing bright blue-green eyes. He worked part-time at the base medical laboratories, and had clearance on base. We started hanging out, and I thought he was safe. When I visited his off-base living quarters, I realized his home did not match the income of a lab technician.

Randy was fun, threw great parties, and I suspected he dealt drugs. Guam is a foothold for the influx of drugs into the US market. I know there was a huge issue with the availability of drugs on island. From my experience with all the young military guys and the gangs I dealt with at school, I understood that many on the island wished to augment their reality; I surmised Randy made extra income from supplying the need. We were never anything but buddies. I think I served as some sort of cover for him on base. Yes, he held a job there, but hanging out with the daughter of the commanding officer also boosted his image on base.

One night I joined him on some type of delivery or pick up or exchange. I was told to wait at the boat for him and his people as they went to do their business. They all came running back down the dock after a short spell. Randy literally picked me up and threw me into the boat as gunfire erupted around us. The guy driving the boat gunned the engine, and off we went, the saltwater spray splashing us in the hasty departure. I have no idea what transpired or where exactly we were. All I knew is that someone was shooting at us, and that my collision with the boat console had cracked a rib. It hurt to breathe deeply and even worse to laugh, which is what we were all doing as the driver slowed the boat down far from shore. I wasn't afraid but exhilarated. As for my broken rib, I knew it just needed well-applied bandaging. Fortunately, I worked with people who could help me with that.

Adrenaline can feel wonderful and addictive, too. Despite having just escaped bodily injury from gunfire, Randy and the others were relaxed and actually laughing. Clearly this wasn't their first rodeo. Their calm and laughter were contagious. I sat slumped in the bottom of the boat, reflecting on the choices that led me here. I wanted to be like my father: Achieve. Behave. Conform. Perform. My mother, however, was cheerfully rebellious and later totally unpredictable with her addictive behaviors. There was a real tension between the two opposite poles presented to me as a child. I was caught in the middle without knowing what the middle looked like. I was either following the rules of predictability or inviting danger into my life so I wouldn't suffocate. I was completely bifurcated into two different people. Was I finding myself here? Was I trying to define who I was by this reckless behavior? Metaphorically speaking, I would find myself back on this boat for most of my life.

Over coffee one morning, my father offhandedly mentioned that someone on base was dealing and that they were very close to catching them. I immediately stopped seeing Randy. My father doesn't offhandedly drop any information. He knew. I would never intentionally embarrass my father, so that put an end to it.

Surviving off base required vigilance. I was always on alert as I was an outsider here on so many levels. I feared for my safety unless I was on the base or visiting other military facilities. I did not drive to destinations in the same way every time. I varied my routes and schedules. I did not enter the high school or community college campus the same way every day nor leave the same way I arrived. I changed my paths between classrooms constantly to avoid being ambushed. Walking to class one day, a boy accosted me and began to taunt me and rip at my clothing much to the delight of his group of friends. I must have caught him off guard when I lashed out at him as he crashed to the ground on his butt. His friends laughed even harder, but I knew I was really in trouble now. Despite all my precautions he caught up with me in a stairwell one day with his friends and his knife. He pushed me into a corner and held the knife to my throat while whispering to me in Chamorro what he was going to do to me. I rather wish I didn't understand him at that point, but he was so menacing I doubt it would have made a difference. I had a knife in my purse, and I had my hand on the hilt. I decided he'd at least get stabbed through my purse even if he cut my throat.

About that time, a security guard came down the stairs whistling. I honestly believe he was whistling because he saw the situation and wanted to give the group the chance to disband before he arrived—oh geez, the paperwork required for this situation. He just kept whistling as he went down the stairs, walking right past us as if nothing was happening. The knife disappeared, the boys faded back, and I ran. I never heard anything more about that entire incident, and I think somehow the boy was happy I didn't file a report somewhere and got him into trouble. Possibly he just found another person to torment.

CHAPTER 11

The Morgue

My last location for vocational learning was the morgue. Would I see bodies, I wondered? What was it going to be like? Would I be afraid or nauseous? All these things raced through my seventeen-year-old brain, but I never shared these thoughts with anyone. When I first arrived, I walked into a lab set up for the coroner to arrive. There were opaque plastic containers containing who knows what. I needed to know before the coroner showed up. What if I was going to lose my mind when he opened a container? What if I fell to the floor nauseated? I had not the foggiest idea what was in those containers, but I set about looking in every single one and putting it back in its original position before I could be discovered. I found tissue of various sorts, biopsy samples, and excised tissue from surgeries. It was no big deal to me. Insert a sigh of relief. I patiently waited until the coroner arrived and began meticulously going through the material, his foot on a pedal to operate a machine which recorded his voice, as he described his findings in amazing detail. How could he discern all that from that piece of tissue he was holding? I was in awe. Eventually I graduated to being allowed to see the bodies, and he performed autopsies. He watched me ever so closely, but I suspect neither of us knew what happened to me inside. All I know is that many of the bodies I saw were victims of violence. I don't know at what age or if there even is an age where one becomes able to view what humans do to each other. It was devastating. Remember to downplay the seriousness of any situation. Pretend everything was normal in my horribly abnormal and dangerous world.

If I had the opportunity to be alone with a body even for a brief moment, I would just hold their hand and let them know they were loved. I never let anyone see this or told anyone about my secret little ritual because I knew they'd think I was crazed. I kept it to myself like everything else.

At that time, we were seeing many cases of dementia in the local population and were busy trying to do the anatomical studies of the brain to see if anything could be discerned to explain this phenomenon. They flew in neuroanatomists and neurosurgeons from Japan and other places to help. I spoke with many families of the deceased gathering their permission to use tissue and bodies. It was challenging. The majority of the people on the island are Catholic, and their religion does not allow for removal of tissue or disturbing the deceased in any way. Later I read about the eventual outcome in *Science* while I was at the university in the early 80s. They believed that this particular dementia was caused by a toxin in the fruit of a cycad tree, the false sago palm. Fruit bats ("flying foxes") eat that fruit and bioconcentrate its toxins; fruit bats are widely consumed by the indigenous people, thereby passing the toxin to humans.

One of the coroner's assistants I worked with had an unfortunate resemblance to the nurse who sold organs in the 1978 movie *Coma*. She rather spooked me, but she was pleasant enough and was a good teacher. I learned how to handle human tissue, embed it in paraffin, and microtome or slice it for examination. All this was done without the protection now deemed necessary for handling human tissue.

I began to have nightmares that tied the morgue to high-school experiences. I would go to work and turn back the sheet only to find the waiting dead body to be me, with my throat slashed by the guy at school with a knife.

CHAPTER 12

Trophy

My physics class was wonderful. The teacher, a wisp of a woman, was exceedingly bright and challenging. When we were doing experiments with light and water, there was a cardboard box in the front of the class which held little plastic containers to hold water such that we could shine light through at various angles. The class sprang into action, gathered the multitude of available huge roaches in the classroom, put them in the little plastic containers, capped the boxes, and replaced them in the bigger box before the teacher arrived. The only person surprised was my lab partner who was late to class. The teacher looked into the cardboard box, and with a wry look on her face, told us to come up and retrieve a container for water.

When my teacher had to take some time off because of thyroid issues, we were given a substitute teacher, Tony, a Chamorro man. He knew nothing of physics, but he did play football for the community college. He was to babysit us and feed us lessons supplied by our teacher in her absence. I think he must have been twenty-six to my seventeen years, and I soon found myself meeting Tony on the beach to walk or play volleyball with his friends.

There was nothing sexual about the relationship. Tony had a girlfriend, but he wanted me to be his date at athletic events where he could show off his new trophy—me. This was my introduction to being second fiddle. I would drive over to his girlfriend's apartment to pick him up, and off we would go. I met her. She was stunning, but I have no idea what she felt about the whole arrangement with her boyfriend and me. I liked it because it further opened up my socializing with all of Tony's older friends who were of all different ethnicities. I particularly loved the Filipinos who delighted in teaching me some of their language, Tagalog. Additionally, I felt safe off the base as long as I was accompanied by Tony or his friends. I knew they would look out for me. I also noticed the tattoo between Tony's thumb and forefinger was the same as the tattoo worn by the crew of guys that menaced me in the stairwell. I absently wondered if this had anything to do with them deciding to leave me alone.

One night while Tony and I walked down the beach, we crossed paths with a group of Chamorro men who had a lot to say about the pairing of the obvious Caucasian woman with the Chamorro man. Tony didn't respond at all, but I let out a barrage of insulting Chamorro in response. What they said about me was demeaning and insulting; I would not have it. Tony just stopped, his mouth agape. Oh wow, he had no reason to think

I spoke or understood anything but English and the bits and pieces of Tagalog I picked up from his friends. The spell was broken. I was no longer a treasured trophy but a woman with a mind and plans of her own. Heaven forbid. We rarely saw each other after that.

Lolin's house was down by the USO. I often stayed there. Yes, it had working plumbing, but you could see the beach and the water through the holes in the floor. I never investigated where the plumbing was connected, but I am fairly certain a good portion of the island did not have proper sanitation. Most of the indigenous people fished for a living, and it was convenient to live close to the ocean. There was another part of the population that found jobs at the huge military bases cashiering, stocking shelves, or doing other tasks.

My parents and I used to go to a special beach called Naval Facility (NavFac), a pristine location on the northwestern coast of the island which belonged to the military and had very restricted access due to its location near other items of interest. One drove out into the jungle and suddenly there were some sentries with very serious-looking weapons and mirrors to look under your car. You'd step out of the car, have your ID checked, car inspected, and you were free to continue. You drove further through more jungle and reached the beach and these remote campsite locations with a primitive grill to make a fire and cook. I never saw another person on that beach, not a speck of garbage, nothing. White sand, blue water, and no humans as far as the eye could see. It was simply stunning. The diving was amazing, and I still treasure some of the shells we found there. We'd bring chicken to cook and the monitor lizards in the jungle would smell it and come to investigate. We even had one gingerly reach out and steal a piece off the BBQ as we quietly sat and watched.

The beaches were irresistible, and I would try to go as often as possible. I kept my gear in the back of the truck. Once out of the water, often the easiest thing to do was use one of the occasional showers (shower heads affixed to a cement out-building) to rinse the salt off your body and gear. The sun and heat dried you so fast, it was just more comfortable to rinse off. I stopped doing this, however, when one day when I was rinsing off I opened my eyes to find I had gathered an audience just standing there and watching me. It was definitely an ick moment. I felt like some woman that I'd seen in those peep shows, only this time, it was unintentional. I quickly gathered my things and left feeling terribly unsafe. In the future I just rinsed my gear at home and let the salt dry on my skin and hair.

Guam is a rabies-free island which means that if you bring an animal with you, they will need to stay in quarantine for a period of time to make sure they do not carry rabies before being released to you. As a result, many people decide to adopt animals on the island rather than transporting their animals to Guam from their original home. Unfortunately, when it is time to leave, many people also abandon their animals. The number of strays, particularly dogs, is astounding. Their media constantly covered this story asking whether the dogs should be rounded up and possibly euthanized. The Filipino population offered to take them because they have no issue with consuming stray dogs. This caused an uproar, but why should we judge anyone for following their culture? After all, it was typically

Caucasians who abandoned these animals. I remember driving to school with a garbage truck directly in front of me slowing traffic. It came to a sudden stop, and a passenger jumped out, put his cigarette in his mouth, reached down with his right hand to pick up the dead dog in the middle of the road, tossed it unceremoniously into the garbage truck, took a drag off his cigarette with the same hand, and waved at me as if to say, "Thank you for waiting". It felt weird, but different strokes for different folks, right?

CHAPTER 13

The Caves

I was invited to go "boony-stomping" with a group of friends and other people. Boony-stomping is an affectionate term for hiking in the jungle. Evidently there was a cave that someone had heard about and wanted to explore. It sounded like fun. At that time, I imagined caves to be big, open spaces carved out of the side of a mountain or rock. We hiked for a while, and when everyone stopped, I didn't realize we had arrived because I couldn't see a cave. The cave was underneath us. Ahead of us a knotted rope dangled down into a hole in the ground; the other end was attached to a nearby tree. I thought, "You've got to be kidding me", but several people walked up to the hole, held onto the rope and disappeared below. You could hear their voices from far, far away.

I didn't know whether I could do this. However, I was determined that no one was going to know that this whole scenario had me spooked. I never said a word. When it was my turn, I walked up to the rope and let the knots thread through my hands as I lowered myself into this immense darkness where I could see little lights, the flashlights of those that went ahead of me. My feet touched what felt like sand. I looked around with my flashlight. The cave was vast, and people wandered around with their flashlight beams leading the way.

I walked over to one side and found big pools of water against the rock cave wall. Little fish swam in the pools of water, and I wondered if it was salt or fresh water. I dared not taste it to find out. I remember squatting there in the dark, my flashlight beam illuminating the tiny fish. I envied them. All hidden here in this massive cave, deep in the dark underground, peaceful, all in their little community. I wanted to be one of them.

Much later in life, I'd find myself in a cave once again, finding peace and connections I didn't know I'd lost.

CHAPTER 14

Social Occassions

My father would occasionally receive gold-leaf invitations, the kind that said you will be here at this time, on this day, and you will wear dress whites (sword and all). This is so not my father. We would go to these extravagant embassy parties and my mother and I would try to behave. We would get the giggles over any silly thing, but mostly we would keep it together and make small talk with the other attendees there to honor whatever we were there to honor. The food was simply amazing, so it was always worth playing dress-up and supporting my father. He would occasionally come over to my mother and me to make some wisecrack or quip which left us sputtering and looking at the floor in the hopes of keeping it together. He would wander off in total innocence. I suppose it was his way to let off steam at such occasions, reminding us that it just wasn't all that serious.

When various ships visited, my father would invite their officers and crew over to our house for big parties. These events were always immensely entertaining because you could watch the interactions of the officers and the crew from different countries and talk about all sorts of things. I particularly remember the parties with the Japanese crews and their commanding officers. I think this is where my love affair with Japan may have begun. The crew was so proper and so polite, and they would watch their officers closely for any sign they were overstepping proper etiquette or losing face. The intricate dance they all did without even saying anything was quite amazing. I loved talking to them and answering their endless questions about everything from Disneyland to how to eat barbeque chicken properly. The crew members were barely older than I was, so we always found lots to talk about.

One of our favorite dance spots was at The Reef Hotel. When a new band showed up with a definite funk vibe, it was a real treat. Because I was there a lot with my friends, I got to know the boys in the band. They were great fun, and we stayed up to all hours of the morning eventually ending up at a McDonald's which was open all night and had Pac-Man consoles. They slept during the days while I worked and went to school. The band leader (drummer) wanted to experience snorkeling, so lessons began and so did the beach picnics. My mother would occasionally come out with me and my friends to go dancing. I'm sure she wanted to experience something outside her little circle of officer wives and luncheons. Her life was so structured and controlled. I was happy to oblige, as she got along easily with my friends, and the guys in the band loved her. She was closer to their ages, loved to dance, had all sorts of music knowledge, and had great stories as well.

She was out with me one evening when we had a run-in with a drunk, obnoxious bar customer. The band, on break, ended up getting involved in the ruckus. I was trying to calm things down as the guitarist, a former Marine, had the customer by his collar and the back of his shirt. This guy was going over the edge of the stairwell into the pool unless we could intervene. I had visions of the police and hotel security arriving on the scene, all of us trying to sort this out—racially mixed band members, some gender-ambiguous individuals, two blonde women, and drunk customers. I knew we'd end up at a police station—some place my father told me never to go. Our group might not ever be allowed to leave. My father would be called if we were lucky. He was at home thinking my mother and I were at the movies or something. It took a lot of begging, but we all walked away. Nobody went swimming unexpectedly. Triumph. My mom and I got home that night and crawled under my bedcovers fully clothed. My father peeked in at us later to make sure we were home. We didn't move a muscle.

CHAPTER 15

Oregon, Part 2

My time in Guam was winding down, and I needed to return to the US to go to college. My plans were to go back to North Bend, get my diploma, live with Ted, get my waitress job back, and work all summer until I started at the university. I was valedictorian of my class, and it came with a scholarship for the University of Guam. I, obviously, wasn't going to college on-island, so I passed that honor to the next available candidate. Lolin got her wish and came back with me. She escaped her little island prison. My right hand had regained total function, ulnar nerve totally recovered, and I had no lasting effects to remind me that my nervous system needed me to pay attention to my stress level. I quickly forgot it had even occurred.

I don't know why I thought anyone in North Bend would be happy to see me when I returned. They didn't much care for me before I left, and now I looked like I had been living in some island getaway—tanned with shockingly sun-bleached hair. If I didn't fit in before, now I was just an insult to their senses. Although I already had a diploma from Guam and another lofty-looking certificate from their community college for all my vocational work, I still wanted a diploma from stateside. I entered into conversations with my old high school in North Bend to further this end. The staff hemmed and hawed and made excuses. It seemed they weren't really interested in helping me, and then they said they'd have to have a student assembly to discuss it. Did the students want me to graduate with them? I could see where this was going, and said no thank you. I'm already done, so never mind. I don't need anyone's approval.

As it turned out, I have never walked at or attended any of my graduations: high school, college, or graduate school. At this point, I couldn't even locate those documents. I was never one for that pomp.

I got my job back waiting tables and moved in with Ted. His apartment was in an old house that overlooked the parking lot of a convenience store. We set Lolin up just down the street in her own apartment. At first, we spent a fair amount of time to-gether, but Lolin quickly made friends in her new surroundings and kind of disappeared from my life. I worked as much as I could, typically double shifts every day, and survived on toasted peanut butter and jelly sandwiches.

Ted had a very busy social life and work, so we just kind of stayed out of each other's way. I did, however, meet one of his friends, David. He was my first real romantic interest. David seemed so grown up, but he had some real trauma in his life with separated parents, his mom on psychiatric meds which I recognized from my mother's experience, and a father who was depressed and isolated.

PART TWO

The Lost Years

CHAPTER 16

Prior to this point in my life, I had been marking time by location, which military base I lived on, and where my father was stationed. I was baggage or luggage brought along on each new move, packed, unpacked, and re-packed along with the clothes and the dishes. Once in college in one location for an extended period, time lost meaning for me as I became laser-focused on school, accomplishing, and achieving. I thought at first I was escaping my father's shadow by not living at his location, but I still conformed to all of his rules and expectations.

I began a new chapter in my life with a feeling of freedom and autonomy.

Decades later, that chapter ended with the loss of my career, health, and mobility. In between was chaos. Driven to over-achieve but colliding with the expectations of others, my young adulthood dissolved into a blur of academia, work, stress, fatigue, and self-neglect.

I started college in the fall. Not many of the people who went to the high school I attended in North Bend went to college, but I recognized my Army-brat friend at New Student Orientation. We took a room together, but she moved out with friends within a short period, leaving me alone in the dorm room. I thought this was great as my roommate was into partying while I preferred to study. It turned out my room was situated on the party floor of the dorm. This was not optimal, so I rode the bus back to Ted's every weekend so I could study. I was advised to take twelve to fourteen credit hours per term to see how I handled it. I was bored, so I quickly increased the number of classes I was taking until I was soon taking twenty-four credit hours per term.

When I started college with scholarships, I knew that I was required to enlist in Work Study to show appreciation for the monies I received for coursework. I was thinking of working in the library or the dormitory cafeteria or something like that. I never supposed that I would end up being responsible for a class in Women's Studies. Saying I was responsible is a bit much because I was only the person who took attendance and filled out the necessary paperwork for the class, but the class itself was something I had never imagined. It was a meeting of a group of women to tell stories, gain support, and discuss whatever topics they chose. I was in awe of these women, all older than my eighteen years, who would openly share their stories, successes, and failures. I was fascinated by what they said, and by their ability to gain support from others. I didn't feel I had anything worthy of sharing, so I just listened intently. The classes always ended late because nobody wanted to leave this secure little bubble, and I always had to run diagonally across campus to the opposite corner where my next class was held. It was a massive room full of seemingly identical chemistry students, heads bent, taking notes, the exact opposite of the friendly, warm, comforting atmosphere of those sharing women. I had to shake myself from the trance of the Women's Studies discussion group to focus on chemical equations and math.

I picked up a job waiting tables with the same franchise I'd worked for previously, and my tips were always very generous. I must have excelled at my job as I was soon training other people, and my supervisor paid me to travel to the biggest restaurant which she oversaw to work and do employee trainings. The pay was lucrative, but my schoolwork was always with me. I studied or worked; no play for me. I also catered banquets for the county at conferences or company events. I tried to get a job at the hospital to no avail. They didn't believe me when I told them what I had been doing in Guam, which I found annoying but unsurprising. I volunteered instead.

My parents were still in Guam, so when the first year of college ended, I needed a home. Ted remained a long bus ride away at this point. I moved in with David who had been transferred to the bigger city where I was attending college. We had a cheap apartment overlooking a parking lot. Our relationship was one of constant turmoil, arguments, and anger. His lonely, desperate father constantly called on the phone wanting to talk with his son; his mother, drugged out on whatever new meds her doctors had her on for depression and anxiety, tried to insert herself into our messed-up lives in her constant search for attention. I cautioned David on his curt and mean-spirited dealings with his father. He ignored me or told me to butt out. His father eventually took his own life. I wasn't surprised, but the event made David even more cold, withdrawn, and angry while drastically increasing his alcohol consumption. I tried to keep things calm and non-confrontational, but what exactly do any of us know at eighteen years old?

David was out drinking a lot with his co-workers and friends, but I had plenty of studying. I needed time to focus and study, not argue or become distracted by his increasingly erratic behavior. One evening, I was at home with dinner on the table waiting for David. He returned home late, again, after drinking with friends, forgetting that we had planned to eat dinner together. I threw everything on the table including dinner plates out into the parking lot. The resentment kept building up. I'd come home from studying at the library for hours, looking like hell, sleep-deprived, stressed, and hungry, and would be met with a drunk accusing me of being out on the town or fornicating wildly with someone else.

Looking back, I should have left at that point. I know I had my own demons to battle when it came to doing enough and being worthy of anything. Instead of leaving, I fixated even more on school and began taking summer courses as well. According to the class schedules, I could take calculus and organic chemistry in the summer rather than spending three terms on these subjects during the school year.

CHAPTER 17

We ended up moving into a rental house, a step up from the apartment, but our problems followed us there. David was convinced I was seeing someone. With my backpack of books seemingly surgically attached to me, three jobs, and a full course load, I didn't have time for his nonsense let alone anyone else's. Still, things spiraled out of control into violence with him threatening to hit me and then slamming the door so hard against the wall that the doorknob punched through the wall. Eventually, all of our walls had holes where the doorknobs hit or he punched through them. He pounded the steering wheel in the car in anger so many times that the horn no longer functioned. He knew if he did anything physically harmful to me, Ted would kill him. I think that's the only thing that stopped David from going further.

Little did I know that his imaginings of my infidelity were just a reflection of what he was doing in his own life. I was too busy to even consider such things. Then one finals week, in my second year of college, David decided he was moving out of the rental house and packed his car and left.

I called my parents who lived thirty minutes outside of town, where they moved after returning from Guam; my father dealt with everything while I studied for finals. He boxed up all of my stuff and moved it out to a spare room at their place while I had my nose deep in the textbooks.

I didn't process why David left or why he was unfaithful. In my mind, I simply didn't have the luxury of going down that path. But my nervous system was registering the effects of living in constant fear. Throughout my life, I'd always felt under threat; it continued through my time in Guam. Those felt like external threats. Now, the threatening flavor came from places and people familiar to me. "Be cautious of everything around you, even the familiar" was much worse than expecting "stranger danger." I was living with the constant threat of physical and mental abuse in my relationship, and the non-stop stress of college. Sitting still in class, my body seemed to hum with energy like I was attached to an electrical current. Loud noises made me jump, and I was overly nervous, hypervigilant, and agitated. I was sleep-deprived, but aren't all college students? I believed my issues were "normal," the things everyone deals with in one way or another.

CHAPTER 18

I met Melissa that summer in Organic Chemistry. I was working at the very end of the lab bench near the ventilation hood where chemicals were stored and dispensed. We were using hazardous chemicals for some simple experiment. Students were to dispense chemicals in the hood for their experiment and carry it back to their station. The class had been warned repeatedly about the dangers of one compound we were using: its breathing hazards, how it eats through gloves and skin all the way to your bones. I always felt that teaching through knowledge and respect was better than teaching through fear, but I didn't teach organic chemistry. What did I know? I was doing my experiment when I heard Melissa behind me at the hood. I don't remember the sound or word she made, I only felt her panic and terror. I turned to see her standing in front of the hood, her outstretched gloved hands covered in the bright red-brown color of the chemical. Others had been careless and dripped liquid onto the outside of the bottle; when she moved the bottle, her hands became covered with hazardous material. I calmly reached for the open ends of her gloves at her wrists and pulled. Each glove inverted itself rendering them harmless and ready to be dropped into the appropriate trash. I moved her to the sink and thrust her hands under cold running water. She was unharmed. I momentarily felt transported back to the ER in Guam, calmly handling challenging situations without panicking and without upsetting the patient. Downplay the seriousness of any situation. Pretend everything was normal in my horribly abnormal and dangerous world.

Our friendship solidified and grew as we spent more time together. We studied relentlessly and partied when we allowed ourselves. We kept lawn chairs in the back of my car and were famous for driving about an hour to the coast at a moment's notice to sit on the beach to unwind. We were incredibly driven but also incredibly spontaneous. We used the old Psychology building and its mazes of rooms to find a quiet place to study. We'd use the whiteboards or chalkboards to lay out problems and study for hours upon hours only to then drive to the coast and share a bottle of wine at the beach.

Melissa and I had equally dysfunctional families; we both had unhealthy relationships with alcohol and the need to over-achieve and be accepted. We were a couple, so to speak, and we didn't have other friends. No one around us was as crazy or studied as voraciously as we did. We just saw things the same way and were incredibly close.

After my second year of college, I was chosen to teach part of the Summer Science Experience (SSE). It is a program for gifted high school students held every summer on campus. It is designed to be a taste of college life; the kids are housed and fed in a dorm, have classes in the sciences, arranged play time like swimming or bowling, and are supervised by the teaching staff at all times. I taught the biology portion on the courses which means designing and arranging courses, labs, lectures and procuring supplies. It was fabulous because these kids were highly motivated and terribly smart. They really wanted to be there. I taught a lot of courses as a student, and teaching remains one of my favorite things to do. The difficulties in dealing with teaching at the university level is the egos of the faculty members and not with the students, I found.[2]

When it was time to take Graduate Record Exams, Melissa and I went to the coast and rented a room to study and look at the ocean. We'd wander the waterfront to buy crab, bring it back to the motel, melt butter on the baseboard heater in a cleaned

---

[2]I taught a lot of courses as a student, Biology for Non-majors, to various other biology courses which were typically taught jointly by a group of professors. I loved teaching. but I could have easily done without the mechanics of dealing with seating charts for a 300-seat room, and personality conflicts of a group of professors. Often the most common question was, "What do I have to do to get an A?" from the pre-med students. Another favorite teaching job was for Evolution and Ecology, the fourth term of the biology core. The first three terms weeded down about 300 students to the last 30-50 survivors. The class included field trips with the students to the mountains and the coast to count trees and crabs, respectively. It was life-fulfilling work which I still consider to be play. You learn a lot about your students as everyone is wading around in the surf setting a line to mark specimen quadrants for crab counts. Too fun!

ashtray, and spread out a towel for our feast. I honestly don't remember which one of us did it, but somehow the table covered with our study material and multitude of applications etc. was ceremoniously set on fire. I guess we tired of the process as we then went out to an old honky-tonk bar in this tiny coastal town and took over the dance floor much to the dismay of the inflexible regulars. I don't think they'd ever seen two women dance together before.

Just before Melissa left for grad school we decided to drive to Canada, stopping at her brother's house on the way. It was pretty uneventful until we arrived at her brother's and stayed up drinking in his Jacuzzi. I recall watching the water climb higher on her face as she slipped asleep into the water, and I pulled her out. We were really drunk, and the morning came much too soon. I was driving, and I knew we'd reached Canada when the speed limit signs changed to kilometers. Melissa sat in the passenger seat with a calculator, frantically figuring out how fast I could go, and couldn't keep from laughing; I'm sure our blood alcohol level was still unacceptably high. At least that day, we had gotten away with our study-hard-party-hard hijinks. I wouldn't always be so lucky.

***

Later, I found myself working as a research assistant for the professor who taught my Comparative Anatomy and Embryology course. I loved being in the lab and was there as often as possible. A friend of mine was getting married, and I drove out to her house, a home in the country just outside of town, for the wedding. The guests put their keys in a basket as we knew there was going to be a lot of drinking. I didn't put mine in as I didn't plan on drinking; I had timed experiments to return to at the lab. On the way back to the lab at a small intersection, I narrowly avoided a guy running a stop sign to enter traffic as he left a mobile home park. I veered to the left, my eyes on him, but unfortunately the car in front of me had stopped to avoid a different hazard. I had veered, but only enough to avoid the car getting ready to T-bone me and not the back rear bumper of the stopped car I had not seen. My seat belt kept me in the car, but I broke the steering wheel with my mouth. I got out of the car, stuffed a rag in my mouth to soak up blood, pointed at the guy who had run the stop sign who was stopped to my right, and went to the car in front of me to check on them. They were fine, but when I looked up from checking on them, the guy who ran the stop sign was gone. The next car that came by picked me up and drove me to the hospital.

Once I was admitted to a room, I took my jewelry off to wash in a barf basin full of water. Then I sat on the exam table, examined the multitude of drawers in the room, reached out for one, and magically found a phonebook inside. I somehow knew where I could find one in the emergency room? Weird. I started looking for dentists. Here I was in the ER, fresh from a car crash, still living by my father's 7Ps, and the mandate to Achieve. Behave. Conform. Perform and taking charge of my next problem. I stopped the search only when the doctor came in to examine the damage and start stitching up my mouth and lips.

I was constantly exhausted but never admitted it. If I had a
talk to deliver or a class to teach, I would just crawl on top of
my desk at work in the lab and go to sleep for a few minutes
beforehand. I was almost immediately in REM sleep which told
me how sleep-deprived I really was. I called these combat naps.
This was, unfortunately, normal for me at this point in my life.
I couldn't fathom how to get out of the position I was in and
believed the way out was to move forward, to get through it all.
I didn't know I could just stop. I now realize the only person I
was fighting was myself, and my constant struggle with being enough, being worthy, and doing enough to satisfy those
around me. The limbic system clearly still felt it was in flight or
fight mode constantly.

CHAPTER 19

I took the highest-level biology course offered at that time, a 500-level course, Electron Microscopy.[3] I fell in love with the machines, the optics, and the hours in the dark uninterrupted. I was fond of the instructor too, and we began dating after the course finished.

Jim further sparked my science-loving analytical brain. We had lengthy, intense conversations, and he encouraged me to expand my horizons in optics by learning photography. We had ample darkrooms and materials in the lab, so it was easy and

---

[3]Electron Microscopes (EMs) are specialized microscopes that use a focused beam of electrons (rather than photons as used in light microscopes) to "image" the specimen and gain information about its structure. Electrons are scattered by heavy metals or compounds, so specimens may be treated with specific heavy metals in order to glean enhanced information about the sample.

fun to branch out and begin looking to the world around me as an avenue to learn about f-stops, apertures, and shutter speed. This further expanded my knowledge of optics and microscopy as well.

Jim was many things, but honest was not one of them. I didn't question anything at first; I was totally unsuspecting. I was unaware he was just shy of my father's age, but I was still looking for someone I believed could keep me safe at that time. Our relationship was about power and money. Soon, I met his two kids. His son was incredibly tempting; I didn't know that he was much closer to my age than his father was. There was definitely electricity between us, but I behaved. Jim was oblivious. I had no idea what his son might think or feel.

Also around that time, I was active in a group supporting the use of animals in medical and biological research. This could be rather aggressive and hostile work with protesters screaming at you, death threats by mail, and checking under your car for bombs. The Animal Liberation Front and People for the Ethical Treatment of Animals, both groups known to promote violent activities to attain their goals, were incredibly active in the city and campus. I did speaking engagements, media interviews, wrote letters-to-the-editor pieces with my hospital connections, and even obtained an iron lung to speak about polio and the resulting vaccines at different events. I infiltrated the campus animal-activists group to learn their methods and obtain literature. This all resulted in me doing speaking engagements for the Foundation for Biomedical Research, The Primate Center, and various hospitals and campuses as well.

I attained my Bachelor of Science in Biology. My father commented, "That with 25 cents and you'll get a cup of coffee." Seventeen years after wanting to be shipped to Vietnam with a box of cookies, and continually working as hard as I could, I still wasn't doing enough to warrant his attention or praise. Hadn't I adhered to the mandate, Achieve. Behave. Conform. Perform? What more could I do?

***

I was the teaching assistant for the electron microscopy (EM) course. There is a huge difference between teaching non-majors to use a lab notebook and observe critters in various aquaria, and teaching upper-division biology students to use heavy metals, epoxy resins, and other dangerous substances to prepare tissue for microscopy. I was very lucky to have such great mentors as my early teachers, and I was determined to be the same for my students. Here I had the opportunity to follow their example of teaching with awareness and respect, rather than using the fear-based approach I resented during Organic Chemistry. I taught my students to be aware of the chemicals you are using, be cautious, have respect and knowledge, and all will be well. It took great dedication, but it was terribly rewarding. You had to be available 24/7. If the students burned out a filament, lost the beam on the microscope, or needed any sort of help, you were the buffer between them and the professor.

I became enamored of the embryonic visual system of frogs and decided I wanted to do an anatomical study for my master's thesis. Most master's theses are library based, but I wanted to do it differently. Unfortunately, during this time, my thesis advisor decided to go on sabbatical in China. So, I was on my own to figure this out.

I worked incessantly. I had a sleeping bag in my office, off the EM labs, next to an old Siemens microscope. I bathed in the deep sink if I didn't wish to take a break or couldn't because I was running a timed procedure. It took me a year before I finished the experiments and written the thesis. I faxed my thesis advisor in China, to set up my thesis defense upon his return to the States. I wasn't even twenty-one years old. When I finished my thesis, I wrote it up for the graduate school of the university and defended it to my committee to receive my graduate degree. This was followed by writing it up as a scientific paper for a prestigious scientific journal where it was published.

My reality check began when an old flame of Jim's came back. She moved in with him and his kids. He threatened to take my keys to the lab away because I worked too much. My traditional physician was busy prescribing me Tagamet (ulcer meds) for my stomach and telling me to cut back on stress. Instead, I researched the pH of different coffees to find the least acidic, hoping to find something less irritable to my stomach. Years later, when I began seeing a functional medical doctor, I learned that my myriad of digestive issues were caused by the years of antibiotics I took as a child, poor gut motility from repeated Epstein-Barr infections, and fungal dysbiosis of the gut. It had nothing to do with gut acidity. Unfortunately, this wouldn't be the last time where I was misdiagnosed or received dangerously wrong medical treatment.

Old Flame eventually left, and Jim and I settled into some

weird dysfunctional relationship. I continued to have an office in the lab and became the de facto EM lab monitor. I was the person doing most of the science there, so it behooved me to keep stocks of photographic paper out to warm, alcohol bottles full, water distilled, solutions made, Parafilm and Kim Wipes ordered, pipettes washed, ad nauseum. I took a position as a general electron microscopist, but my salary was paid by one principal investigator even though I did work for whomever needed it. My benefactor wanted me to be available to devote all my time to his work at the drop of a hat should he need me to do so. Jim told me I was free to do my own research and that time on the microscope would be free. This, of course, was all in theory until Jim felt threatened by one of my co-authors, and we got into a very heated argument over lunch while at a Cell Biology conference in San Francisco. My co-author offered to pay for lab services I undertook, and I told him to stay out of it if he knew what was good for him. It was all about control.

I eventually moved in with Jim. He kept a 3x5" card on the refrigerator that said T Spent and Jim Spent to keep track of who owed who what each month. I had no idea Jim was going to behave in such a controlling manner at home, but I suppose I might have guessed by similar behavior at work. He was very particular about how he wanted things done and was very opinionated. Much of this was ignored as he was very smart.[4]

---

[4] I'm sure part of the issue was that Jim always felt inferior in an academic setting because he didn't have a graduate degree, and I now had one, too. I can personally attest to the fact that there are many people with higher degrees who exhibit very little intelligence. I've met some of them in academia, in biotech, at conferences, and in classrooms.

We threw lavish holiday parties, breakfasts, or more intimate gatherings for faculty from the university. I'd clean the house and do most of the preparation. During the party, I'd go out onto the deck surrounding the house and peer through the windows at the people partying. I felt like an imposter in my own house, but I met the most interesting people out there on that deck—people like me who just wanted to escape. My favorite drink was Sapphire gin with lime, and I could feel the little bits of lime as they scratched down my throat. I'm sure part of it was for Jim to show his amazing house, with his trophy not-a-wife (me) to all his colleagues. Melissa came back for one of these parties and she was quietly aghast when she saw how excruciatingly thin I was. I saw it in her face. I didn't think I was fat; I just was so stressed that I rarely ate. Drinking was much easier than swallowing food.

***

My sports medicine doctor, Steven, a good friend, one day said simply, "Do you want to see a man or a woman?" I said what? "Therapist," he said. Oh.[5]

I was new to therapy. When my therapist asked how I wanted to start with the physical or mental side, I said don't touch me, the mental side. My father is God and my mother is a drug addict, I recall saying.

---

[5] Steven and I remain good friends. I will always be grateful to him for his gentle guidance and care. He's always had my best interest at heart.

When I had my first panic attack, I was listening to the director of the Sleep Disorder Center at Stanford speak on campus at an event I had organized. I was standing at the back of the room when the first waves hit. I ran outside and walked quickly up and down the sidewalk. When I described this to my therapist, he said it was a normal reaction to bringing up traumatic events. What? "Then let's stop bringing them up," I naively thought. I had other attacks when I was in my toy box with all my stuffed animals, the toy box I had in Helena that my dad built. During the attack, I remembered that my brother Frank used to shove me in the box with my stuffed toys and lock the lid, leaving me to panic inside.

CHAPTER 20

When I was around twenty-six years old, it became difficult to stand up straight, lift my legs to walk, or sit for any length of time. My sports medicine doctor asked for an MRI, and we found a bulging disc. He gave me anti-inflammatories and prescribed lots of exercises and ice. I was now at home prone on the floor with an ice bag on my back most of the time. I refused to have any type of epidural or narcotic pain meds or other extreme intervention. I stopped working for months while I was recuperating. I would put on silly TV shows to entertain myself while doing my exercises. Jim made sure to mention this detail to other people. It seemed spiteful.

I eventually graduated to the Back Care center where there was an entire household set up to teach a back injury patient how to vacuum, unload a dishwasher, and do rudimentary tasks. I was soon back at work, but I still couldn't sit. We modified the equipment in the lab so I could work standing. I bought Sacro-Ease ergonomic back supports for chairs and airplane seats when I could finally sit for short periods. It took about a year to get to this point.

If we were at a Chamber Music Society event and I was speaking to one of the musicians, Jim's hand was on my elbow. He would squeeze it if he didn't like what I was saying. I ignored him. He was having trouble with alcohol; I was also drinking too much. He was belligerent and nasty. I was quiet and brewing.

I believe I stayed in the relationship with Jim because I didn't want to be seen as a failure, and I so wanted to be worthy of something, worthy of a relationship, worthy of an exciting career. I couldn't imagine leaving and trying to figure out what came next. It's what keeps us paralyzed in situations we'd most likely leave. It is more comfortable to stay in the dysfunctional rather than to risk the unknown. Oh geez, I'd have to move, and I'd have to find a new job, and imagine the gossip at the University. Everyone thought things were great in our relationship. Oh, the turmoil of change. My system was on overload. I drank too much, didn't sleep, worked like a fiend, and propped up a persona of someone I was not—a happy half of a power couple.

Melissa, still my best friend, and I met in San Francisco for a short break to decompress which we did by shopping and being ourselves—intense and incorrigible. I met with one of my scientific co-authors in town, but Melissa and I mostly stayed to ourselves, as usual, visiting museums and shopping a lot. While at the Asian museum we were walking a path of stones across a picturesque pond, and I noticed my footing wasn't as precise as normal. Odd, maybe we'd just been walking too much, I thought, briefly. I was meeting my best friend to spend money, buy things I didn't need, drink, and distract myself. My life was a crash site, and I felt like a piece of debris that had yet to be cleaned up.

***

My sports medicine doctor, Steven, and I flirted with the numbness in my legs for some time. Eventually, I couldn't feel them when I shaved which was quite disconcerting, but I didn't want to address it. Being the professional he is, Steven finally suggested I have it investigated. I was twenty-eight years old then. I didn't have time for this; I was a busy woman. My protests were ignored; he got me into a neurologist immediately.[6]

I had an MRI, and then played stupid so I could look at the scans with the tech. What pretty pictures you have there, as he flipped through my brain scans. I didn't have a brain tumor, but I did have a small spot.[7] Was this loss of myelin, the fatty insu-

----

[6]If you can immediately get into a neurologist, unless you know them personally, you probably don't want to see them.

[7]This didn't panic me because I knew spots come and go without symptoms. In random asymptomatic people from the flurry of scans that were originally done with the actual development of the MRI, tons of data was available about this. Spots could be an issue, but it just wasn't necessarily so. I'd actually written an article with a radiologist friend from the hospital to point out that animals were used to develop all these wonderful tools, MRI, PET, CT scans, we now have.

lation around nerve matter or was it an artifact? The tech was horrified as I began to identify the anatomy out loud. Whoops. Thanks, and I was off to walk down the street back to work.

I did not, at this point in time, connect this episode with the right hand issues and weakness of my ulnar nerve in Guam ostensibly due to severe fatigue, a questionable spot on my brain, and leg weakness and numbness. Had I thought about it long enough, I would have had to admit the common denominator was stress in my life. Unfortunately, I was too far in denial at that point to admit there was anything bizarre or dysfunctional about the way I was conducting my life.

Even so, as I walked down the street, I knew I was leaving Jim. I didn't know what the spot meant yet, but it did not matter. I knew I had to go. This relationship was dysfunctional and ridiculous. I suppose I had successfully modeled it after what I had seen with my parents, a control drama.

CHAPTER 21

I returned to the lab to make a follow-up appointment with the neurologist. They said he was busy, and I said I would come to his office and wait until he wasn't which I did. The neurologist was incredibly nervous. He told me I had multiple sclerosis; he was sure of it. He told me that my life was over. He actually said that to me.

I could only think about this doctor's unprofessional manner and absently wondered how he had made it through a class in medical ethics. I asked him for my MRI scans which launched him into new rounds of justifying his diagnosis. I said I didn't care what he thought, but I wanted my scans to make slides for my lectures speaking to the positive points of the use of animals in medicine and its diagnostic tools. He was dumbfounded and just stared at me, mouth agape.

***

I took my films and left to make some phone calls, one of which was to a neurologist I trusted in Portland. I wanted someone else to look at these films.

The trip to Portland was pretty uneventful as spinal taps go. The spinal tap was part of the full work-up my neurologist friend insisted upon to look into my mysterious leg numbness and the MRI films. The doctor was more concerned that I'd picked up some unknown virus or parasite living in Guam and working with human tissue without proper protection. He was also furious with the original doctor for diagnosing me with anything based on films, which were underdeveloped, and an incomplete work-up. He even called the guy to berate him for his lack of professionalism. My spinal tap was clean as were the other tests which were run.

At my insistence, my sports medicine physician ran a literature search at the hospital for me. I started reading the citations and did not like what I found. This was not happening to me, and with that, I closed the journal and stopped researching—which is just the way I was used to operating: gain wisdom in order to make an informed decision and "control" the situation. In this case, though, the information was all depressing, so I decided that wasn't the best avenue. This was not happening to me.

The unfortunate thing was that a great amount of damage had already occurred. People can end up feeling different, isolated, separate, alone, and identified with a story of dis-ease, purely by the attachment of a diagnosis or the labeling of a condition. Even though I was all bluster in the office, demanding my films,

part of me down deep heard the "Your life is over" pronounce-
ment and other downright unnecessary and cruel things that
the neurologist said to me. Part of me, I am sure, believed
what he said. Even though my neurologist friend in Portland
dispelled the previous misdiagnosis with all his own testing,
part of me believed that original proclamation. Coming from a
childhood where I was always told there was something wrong
with me and that it would always be this way, a part of me
accepted that. This was most unfortunate and still haunts me
to this day.

CHAPTER 22

By the fall of 1991, my fatigue had become so severe I entered the hospital for a short course of IV steroids to calm my immune system down and dampen any possible swelling of neurological tissue I may have. My mother came down to help. I was still living with Jim, but he was not the caretaker type. After a short respite of seemingly being okay, I was again having severe fatigue. My long-distance neurologist put me on a longer course of oral steroids during the holidays and told me not to do anything drastic like leave relationships or dye my hair purple. The joys of corticosteroids.

Jim's son, Adam, had just been married in Colorado, but Jim and I hosted his wedding reception at the faculty club at the university. I buried myself in preparation, menus, flowers, and invitations. Adam and I had always been friends, talking at social functions, and meeting for a quiet lunch occasionally when he was on break from college. But we also engaged in outrageously flirtatious behavior when we could get away with it. I still remember him feeding me chocolate-covered strawberries in the kitchen during some party. Naughty and risky, and it was all very confusing. While I recognized I had a definite attraction to Adam, I was trying to not explore that train of thought. I was just trying to get through each day at this point. The day of the reception I had a blinding headache. I managed to get through the evening, but it turned into a migraine by the time I got back to the house.

My maternal grandmother, who lived in town at a care facility, began to decline, and I knew I needed to bring my mom down to town so she could spend more time with her mother. During this time, I would need to stay at Jim's because my mom needed a place to live. This meant me not moving out of Jim's immediately. She moved in with us into one of the rooms downstairs. She heard everything that was going on upstairs. She would hear the crashes and bangs of screwdrivers and other objects hitting the wall. She would hear the yelling and loud arguments. I would come down and tell her to concentrate on her mom. I was waiting to move until her mother transitioned.

My mom and I found an apartment for me to rent. Jim insisted I had a brain disorder. Melissa, still my best friend and confidante, delighted in telling me if I just wore an ice pack on my head things would improve because cooler temperatures help those with neurological issues. I know now I did have a brain disorder (limbic system impairment), just not the one Jim thought I possessed. My grandmother soon left this mortal coil; I drove my mother back to her home and moved out of Jim's house. I was finally free of that constant control, but I was not free of huge stressors. Jim and I still worked at the same lab. Our relationship was amicable. It had to be. We sat on some of the same committees, and I worked in the facility he directed.

***

I began to regain some sensory and motor functions in my right hand that I previously had lost. I spoke to the neurologists about this. No explanation. Neuroplasticity wasn't a very popular idea at that time, but I knew my body was rewiring circuits and repairing. There wasn't any reason, in my mind, that any part of the body can't repair and regenerate even though we were taught this was not the case. Biology, when I attended college, believed only specific parts of the body could make a partial recovery from a biological or mechanical injury. I privately wondered why. I just couldn't believe that all parts of us were not capable of healing with the right motivation, thoughts, input, or structure. I didn't know exactly how that happened, but it was something I firmly believed even in my late twenties. I thought that quite possibly what deterred this healing from happening was our limiting beliefs about what was possible. It's true of anything. If you don't believe you can do it or achieve it, then you can't.

Betaseron was the first drug on the market to supposedly minimize symptoms of multiple sclerosis. It is a beta-interferon, injected subcutaneously, the thought being that it dampen the immune response enough to slow long-term outcomes of disability. I went to the hospital, read the original journal articles, and poured over the science. Well, maybe the science works, but backing up, do I believe my diagnosis? There were just so many "what if" questions. Believing and understanding science the way I did, I made the decision to take Betaseron.

In our lives, we make many decisions that in hindsight we wish we'd made differently. This was one of them. By making this decision, I accepted the label of multiple sclerosis—an inaccurate diagnosis—and began defining what I could and could not do according to the beliefs that accompanied this label. I made this decision through the lens of fear, through many what ifs. As I'm fond of saying now, I could be hit by a bus tomorrow and all the ruminations about what may happen in the future are rendered meaningless. Yet I had been taught that you need to control all aspects of life in order to succeed. I thought I could control my health by making this decision.

CHAPTER 23

When I was twenty-eight years old, I didn't know what would come to pass with Betaseron twenty years later.[8] However, I was well aware that, no matter how much I loved science, I couldn't keep working in the lab with Jim and gain my freedom and independence.

I received a call from the Vice Provost of the university one

---

[8] Over twenty years later, the authors of the papers had to admit the data wasn't as promising as they had hoped. Now that they had a larger data pool of people injecting over a longer period of time, well, it wasn't that convincing. After reading this new study, I remember glancing outside at our front yard and watching our neighbors' kids play in the grass. I thought about going upstairs, grabbing my pistol, and shooting myself, but I didn't want to make a mess in the house. The cats would traipse through the detritus and make an even bigger mess to clean up. Sigh. I wouldn't go outside and create an easier to clean crime scene and traumatize the children either.

day. He wanted me to start working for Veterinary Services, the centralized housing facility for all animals on campus. He chose me because of my continued work and success dealing with the animal activists, my extensive understanding of the regulations concerning the use of animals in research, my scientific knowledge and my familiarity with the science faculty. Also, I think he wanted a poster child--someone who could speak to the need for basic research because they have an illness. Already those around me were using my label to further their own agendas. I really needed get out of the lab, so I jumped at the chance.

I worked on the Institutional Animal Use and Care Committee and as a liaison for all of my scientist friends, but mostly I was a glorified secretary for Monte, a serious control freak. I even had my business cards state my position as Glorified Secretary. There were two vets on staff, but they were not on site. Monte was the director and didn't have even a bachelor's degree. This was academia, so things like this mattered. He was allowed to stay in this position because it was cheaper for the university to have the vets off-site and visit when needed while having a pencil-pusher do the books for the facility. Nobody respected him and continually made fun of him. The public-safety person, a friend of mine from our days of asbestos abatement monitoring on campus, would send me silly video memes of monkeys directly before I had to attend meetings with all aforementioned parties. The grad students and I were considering writing a mystery novel where Monte is murdered with each chapter written by a member of the facility with their own reason and method of ending him.

In this new position, I noticed a pattern, an effect I have on people. It's a dynamic where I won't cave to what they want me to do or what they think I should be doing, and it infuriates them. I could remember moments with my brother Frank, David and Jim here. They became so angry with me because I wouldn't bend—and they would start yelling, angry to the point of violence. Here at this new job, Monte would stand directly in front of me and scream in rage because I didn't agree with him, wouldn't back him in silly power games at the university, or because he embarrassed himself in front of a graduate student. Then, one day, my nervous system gave out, my legs failed, and I collapsed in a heap on the floor as he screamed at me. I remember thinking, "Wow, he doesn't even have a weapon and isn't going to hit me, so how am I supposed to feel threatened?" Intellectually I knew Monte was a total buffoon; yet my body, my nervous system felt threatened enough by his behavior to react. Make light of everything as if it were a joke. Downplay the seriousness of any situation. Pretend everything was normal in my horribly abnormal and dangerous world.

In the end another employee and I filed complaints. Things were just getting out of hand with Monte's controlling behavior and his sexist and racist comments. The staff and Monte then engaged in group mediation with a counselor named Gayle. That enabled us to see Monte's personnel file which was filled with previous employee complaints of the same sort. We didn't believe it would have an effect, but we knew Gayle had to write a final report with her findings at the end of the mediated meetings. The group meetings ended with no progress. The only findings were that another employee was the child of an alcoholic so abhorred any kind of confrontation, and that Monte was an even bigger ass than we could have imagined.[9]

I soon realized that Office of Veterinary Services and Animal Care (OVSAC) was the only place I felt safe—at least when Monte wasn't there. It was the most secure facility on campus, outfitted with a retinal scan and key cards to match the individual and the access they needed. Most people had access during the day or occasionally during the evening if they were running experiments. I always had access. I lived in the facility at night. I took combat naps on the cot, showered there, and spent hours on the web researching the beginnings of neuroplasticity and rewiring of the human nervous system. I felt safe there knowing the hours that others kept, who I was likely to run into when, and the public-safety officers that might come by the facility. I had a software program on my computer that made shared files always available to others, but my personal email required passcodes to view. I felt like a knight within a castle ready for battle, my chainmail on and weapons chosen. This place was my fortress.

My nervous system, although accustomed to the fighting stance, continued to suffer greatly. I was buckling under the pressure, but I was still very good at keeping everything hidden.

---

[9]After leaving that job, I received a postcard from Gayle explaining that nothing was going to be done. Monte's cheap labor in comparison to having someone qualified on site resulted in the university administration being uncompelled by our additional complaints.

Achieve. Behave. Conform. Perform. I continued to try to be worthy by my father's standards. One of my good friends, Stephen, told me I was looking for an honorable death. I laughed at the thought, but I think he was correct.

***

I met Heinrich at the gym. By now, I was clearly an adrenaline junkie, and he just screamed danger in so many ways that I couldn't resist. A friend of mine used to tell me that if I saw trouble walking down the other side of the street, I'd cross the street to give it a $20 bill. It was true.

Once, Heinrich and I attended the wedding reception of a friend of mine. He was dressed up for the occasion and looked like someone who had been hired to entertain the female guests—and entertain he did. He was clearly in his element, flitting between dances with different women, a tango here and a salsa there, and bending down to whisper secrets and trade private conversation. He was the consummate partner to every female. Amazingly good-looking, dashing, and attentive, he danced his way through the evening smiling the entire time.

I stood watching him, amazed as always at his ability to slip between characters and personas in any situation. He was such a chameleon. Nobody present knew him; he was just my partner. Eventually women would approach me, out of breath from dancing and being whirled about, asking if he had any brothers. "Introduce us to more of your friends," they pleaded. "He's just so much fun and so charming," they exclaimed. Umm. No, I thought.

It's important to remember the word "charm" is a verb (and a noun, too). We tend to think of it as an adjective or a descriptor. As a verb, it means to affect by or as if by magic, to compel. I happen to find this the perfect definition for what Heinrich was doing to his dance partners. He was having a wonderful time, but he is an illusionist of sorts. The person the guests saw is who they wanted to see because of his vivacious behavior and NOT who he was.

I knew that none of these women, none of these guests, could deal with the whole that was Heinrich. Yes, he could be great at a social occasion, but he was also dangerous, unpredictable, violent, maddening, mercurial, and cruel. These guests would never see those parts of him. They would not be able to handle those parts, yet somehow, I found it acceptable to be in this situation myself. I'd been suffused in the volatile and chaotic since I was a child. I thought I was different, maybe even special.

Heinrich eventually had to admit he had a problem with alcohol and started going to Alcoholics Anonymous meetings. I went with him to be supportive, but soon realized through the stories of other attendees that I, too, had a problem with alcohol. I was a functioning alcoholic. I never missed work or blacked out, but I used alcohol to try to cope with my life. I never knew what kind of craziness would visit on any given day or time; it was rather like working in the ER in Guam, and I felt comfortable with that. It was a startling realization about the alcohol. I cleared all of the alcohol out of my house, a most embarrassing endeavor when I saw how much I had stashed. I stopped drinking cold turkey with lots of AA meetings, fizzy water, and willpower.

Heinrich was unable to stop even though he tried many different rehab facilities and treatments. It was hard to remain as close to him because he continued to drink, but I also believed leaving our friendship meant that I was betraying him. It finally reached a point, however, when I knew I was putting my own life at risk by staying. Years later, Heinrich did ultimately succumb to alcoholism.

***

At this point in time my right leg was occasionally numb. I would carry a cane in case of fatigue; I mostly used it as a walking stick and not for actual support. Mostly I carried so much anger that I found myself wanting to beat people with it. Bubbling and brewing just beneath the surface, the anger I had cultivated throughout my life was the heat keeping my nervous system on a constant low boil.

I had the very occasional relationship. The man was always dangerous, married, or both. Okay, so one was with an engaged man, but he neglected to tell me he was engaged until we were in some sort of long-distance intimate relationship. We were co-authors, and it really stung that he played me. It ended our friendship and our scientific collaboration. I always told myself it was because my life was so busy that I became involved with such men; I didn't have time for someone to devote all of their attention and wants and needs to me or listen to what was important to me. It wasn't true. All my life I had been told, literally and figuratively, that I was damaged goods, a vase that was now cracked, a kid that constantly needed medical care, a bother, and an impediment to joy. I didn't believe I deserved anyone who would devote all of their attention to me or be interested in mine. I got used to being someone to abandon when they felt our time was up.

My last relationship at the university was with a graduate student. Oh my, he was fun. However, as usual, it was complicated. His girlfriend had abandoned him, or so I was led to believe, and so ensued our dalliance of mutual amusement. I told him that I had a propensity for complicated relationships, and I was done with that, but he assured me his previous relationship was over. I wanted to believe him. When she eventually returned home after her wanderings, they got back together. Maybe that was always the plan?

I wasn't surprised. Disappointed, but not surprised. I asked him into my office, not so I could chide him for his betrayal, not because I was angry with him, but because I needed to finally hear that I needed to stop doing this. I was angry with myself. I needed to be number one. I needed to put myself first. While he sat there and cried, I assured him that I wasn't the least bit angry with him—only with myself for being so willingly blind once again. After all, we had too much fun, but I needed to stop this merry-go-round and get off for good. At that point, I made a pact with the universe to find a man who was right for me, who put me first, who was my partner, who was exclusive to me, and who did not lie to me. I felt like I was in a movie where the heroine finally understands what she has been doing and declares she's through with that nonsense. I asked the universe for a man who would love me for who I am, accept all of me even the most tarnished parts, and I was delivered Adam.

CHAPTER 24

Many years after I had moved out, Jim came over to pick something up. He brought Adam with him; I had not seen Adam in so long, and he gave me a big hug. Wow, I remember thinking, now that felt different. I hugged him again to double-check, and yowza, that was indeed different. That was a real hug with emotion and affection behind it.

I felt a connection with him that was so different from all of that flirting we did previously. I felt like this relationship was worth exploring. Did Adam feel it, too? Could we talk about it as adults and as more than flirty twenty-year-olds? We started emailing over the summer. He was still living in Boulder, was divorced, and we quickly moved up to video chatting and talking on the phone. By November, I was on a plane to Boulder. He doted on me, and I knew I had found where I belonged. By the time our weeklong visit was up, we had made plane reservations for me to come back permanently. I went back to the university to give my two-week notice.

Oh, this was so not going to go over well, I thought to myself. I still sat on committees with Jim, and there were many people who thought they knew what my relationship with Jim of a decade ago was about. Everyone around us believed we had a pretty typical relationship. Far from it, actually. For me it had been about the intellectual bond, the science, the learning, the expansion of my knowledge; for him, I imagine, it was the power he thought he exerted over me, whether it be he believed he was smarter or wealthier (certainly true) or a more cultured individual. It does not matter. I was called any number of things from a kept woman to a mistress when I made my final exit from the university. Whatever.

Before I could leave in good conscience, I had to do something about Monte's misdeeds involving the controlled substances and the DEA logs because only I knew the details. The DEA showed up for a snap inspection on my last day, and Monte blubbered as he tried to pass blame to the principal investigators while I deflected his efforts regarding open vials of Buprenex, missing vials of ketamine, and similar items.[10] I walked out knowing I had whacked a hornet's nest, but I did what I believed was right. I was true to myself. It was a fitting ending to my career in academia.

---

[10]Just for the record, I had reported all of this, to no avail, to the attending veterinarian whose DEA license the facility used, prior to calling my friend in environmental health and safety. I was perfectly happy to have it addressed in-house as long as they did something about it. I tried to play by the rules, but others just wanted to sweep it all under the rug.

PART THREE

Surfacing

CHAPTER 25

Boulder, Colorado

When I moved to Adam's home in Boulder in November of 1999, I left my cats and my car behind at my house with my brother, Ted. I just needed to escape the toxicity which had become my environment—better said, the poisonous atmosphere which I had created.

The day we got home from the airport, Adam and I sat on the couch and just talked. We discussed his failed marriage, what went wrong. We then moved on to Jim, and the lies I was told. I learned that Adam's mother worked at a bookstore near the university and lived locally. (I was told she moved back East with another guy who she left Jim for). We talked about how we wanted our relationship to be, what was important for us--exclusivity with no secrets. I don't even remember when we stopped talking. I know our conversation went on through the night. Neither Adam nor I cared about what came before, his ex-wife, Jim, nothing. We were living in the now. I'd never experienced such joy.

With this healthy, loving relationship with Adam, I thought I had left the cast of players in the toxic environment behind. However, my ever-vigilant limbic system did not receive that memo. My nervous system, accustomed to being fed adrenaline, would not be quieted so easily.

I was finally in an environment where I could relax with no stressors or responsibilities. I had planned to look for work at the local university, but Adam told me I needed to heal and rest. I slept constantly. Sure, I got up to eat and occasionally do something fun with Adam, but mostly I slept and had vivid nightmares of past trauma. This went on for months while my body caught up. I had amazing fatigue, could barely climb stairs, and couldn't wiggle my toes. I remembered the head of the Sleep Disorder Center in Stanford, Dr. William Dement, telling me that our body keeps track of the sleep we miss. We may think we're catching up on sleep we missed during the week when we sleep in on the weekend, but it doesn't work that way. Our body keeps track of every lost minute of sleep, and I was now living proof.

Within a year, I was able to climb stairs with more ease, but it would take me thirteen more years to be able to wiggle my toes again. I also used to be able to pick a tea bag out of a freshly poured cup of boiling water, but now my hand was sensitive to temperature and would no longer allow that. I was regrowing nerves, making new pathways, and repairing damage in my nervous system.

***

In early 2000, during an unusually mild winter, Adam and I flew back to my previous home to retrieve my cats and visit a few friends and some of Adam's family. We had dinner with several of my close friends at a popular Italian restaurant and discussed future plans and current events.

While we were eating, Adam and I noticed his father, Jim, and his current girlfriend on the other side of the dining room. We quietly watched, explained to our friends that we needed to get moving, and exited the establishment without being noticed by Jim.

Once outside, Adam and I dissolved into laughter. I said something to the effect of, "Which one of us asked for that?" Adam admitted that he had toyed briefly with the idea of possibly running into his father while we were back in town. He was the guilty party.

CHAPTER 26

Parenting My Mother, Again

I had left my academic life for good and settled into Boulder. Several years later, Adam and I had developed a love affair with Japan. We traveled there twice a year to see different places from Aomori to Fukuoka, and from Matsue to Sendai.

We loved the attention to nature and spirit, the ancient temples, the hospitable nature of its culture, the rituals of green tea, the smell of incense in the air, and the amazing gardens from landscape to Pure Land Buddhist. Visiting Japan during 2007-2009, I walked long distances without any aid. I believed my body had rewired, healed, calmed down and things were good. In a visit during 2009, though, I noticed my left foot drag occasionally (not the right-side weakness I originally experienced in 1991). My nervous system was reminding me that it was not all quiet inside.

***

During one of our trips to Japan, my mother came down to look after our cats and have a little alone time. When we returned home, she was very ill. We took her to the ER immediately. Seemingly she had an infected tooth in our absence, and the dentist in the area gave her a narcotic for pain and an antibiotic. My mother has never been good at caring for herself, so she didn't eat or drink and just took the drugs which left her severely toxified.

She ended up in the hospital for some time while Adam and I tried to recover from an international vacation—which now wasn't much of a vacation at all—and look after her. The medical care is much better in Boulder than where my folks lived, so she stayed here in the hospital while we searched for a dentist to take care of the infected tooth when she was discharged. The tooth was pulled, and she reverted to the woman of my childhood, drugged up on narcotics, sitting on the sofa falling asleep and tumbling off the furniture.

It became so bad that Adam threatened to leave. I called my dad to retrieve his wife. I felt so guilty. Did I make a mistake? Was she just tired? Was I being oversensitive to my childhood trauma? By the time we got to the meeting point to hand over my mother to my dad, I was distraught. I was close to hysterical and, sobbing, I told my father, "I failed!" This is what I had learned in my childhood and thought throughout my entire life. I failed. I wasn't good enough, didn't try hard enough, didn't do enough; in my eyes, I just simply couldn't win when it came to pleasing my dad.

I look at this situation now, and I wonder how I ever could have thought it was my responsibility to take care of a drug addict, why my father didn't come down and retrieve his wife earlier, and how it had all gone so terribly wrong. Oh, but it was just like when I was a kid, when my dad was on the ship, and I was left with my mother who was either in the hospital or incapacitated or both.

My mother and I didn't speak for about a year. My father went through her suitcase and found ample narcotic prescriptions both filled before she came down and from the dentist she saw here in the area. While Adam and I felt somewhat vindicated in calling an end to the situation, we were left feeling very hurt and used. My mother has never spoken of that occurrence. It is as if it never happened.[11]

---

[11]As I was putting the final touches on this book, my mother came forward to apologize for this incident. She continues on her own journey of awareness. It's all any of us can hope for.

CHAPTER 27

The House Next Door

The house next door to us was a rental. We knew the previous owners, but they moved across town while the wife rented the property to various tenants. She was rarely around to check on the property or how things were going; she got into an unfortunate habit of emailing me for news. The last tenants she rented to were obnoxious and didn't respond to polite inquiries to stop their three dogs from barking incessantly. I began to take note of when the dogs barked on a daily basis, and then I called the police. We were constantly being woken up by the dogs, and this had to stop. This, believe it or not, landed us in city-sponsored mediation. You might imagine what I thought of this after my experience at the university. The important thing to note here is how close these two properties are. I can balance on the deck railing of our property and step to their back deck if I wished. Adam was fearful when grilling dinner because the German Shepherd was so aggressive and believed Adam was within his doggie turf. This dog could have easily jumped to our deck in one bound.

I refused to be physically in the same room with the tenants, so all mediation was done through the mediator in separate sessions. We could tell when the neighbors had a mediation session because the man would come home and stand on his back deck and scream at us. I picked up the phone, called the mediator and allowed her to hear his tirades. Still, in the end, we were all just supposed to politely sign a form, and that was it.

I wouldn't allow this mediation event to go the way of the experience at the university. We were not going to just listen to the renter next door scream and threaten us. We were not going to sit by and wait for someone else to solve the issue. We are going to do something! Once again, a threat had emerged in my environment, and the old behavior—control at all costs—reared its head.

Adam and I decided to buy the rental house next door so we could exert some control on our environment; we did not want to move! We contacted the owners and said we knew interested buyers, and the house was ours without even looking at the inside.

I immediately hired a property manager, Sue, who was recommended by a friend. Despite the fact we hired Sue, I dealt with the majority of property-related issues. The problem was twofold: 1) because we were right next door, Sue tended to depend on us to just run over and do things, and 2) I was a control freak and was always taking on more responsibility. Neither of these things were beneficial to my overtaxed nervous system. The last thing I needed was more to do or consider.

Our relationship with Sue culminated when she hired a friend to do some outside work. He got half-way through the job then quit, claiming he couldn't do more because of the height of the house. Sue called me, livid, and we all met in the front yard. I tore the guy apart verbally for not doing a drive-by before taking the job as was stipulated and then not saying up front that he couldn't do the job. He could have told us then that he couldn't do the work. This embedded behavior was great at fighting and confrontation. Sue just stood and watched me discipline her friend, and I realized in that exact moment that she was having me do her job for her. I immediately stopped my tirade.

Then I remembered that a friend had given me a recommendation for a new property manager. Not long thereafter, Sue announced that she was retiring and we promptly hired the second manager. We never have to deal with the house next door anymore, and we have lovely tenants living there.

After that experience, I began to learn more about my boundaries. These days, I don't undertake anyone else's emotional work or tasks deemed extra. I need to reserve my energy for myself, to heal my overtaxed nervous system. Contrary to what I was taught to believe early in life, there is no need for tirades or screaming, ever. I am learning to choose calm.

CHAPTER 28

Rheumatology

I continued my healing process. In May 2012 I noticed my walking was hampered by my left foot dragging and my trying to swing it around to take a step (leg circumduction gait). This resulted in my hips being off, my right hip, in particular. I ended up feeling constantly sore, and not able to get very far without tripping or hanging onto objects in the house.

I obtained a WalkAide, a medical device to assist me with walking. We named it Oscar, after Oscar Goldman of *The Six Million Dollar Man*. With this medical device, I was able to achieve much greater independence.[12]

Using the WalkAide had a cost, though. I was forcing my leg to work through overstimulation while not listening to what my body was trying to tell me—namely, slow down. I noticed sores appearing on my calf under Oscar's electrodes. I was not amused. I'd try to let them heal by not wearing Oscar, but my mobility issues remained challenging. If I couldn't use Oscar, I couldn't get around and do things by myself.

I stopped wearing Oscar when the sores persisted, and I began to get edema or swelling in my lower leg. I was clearly changing the lymph drainage by Oscar's constant constriction just below the knee.[13]

Rather than paying attention to what my body was trying to tell

---

[12]I started with a brace or ankle-foot orthosis, but for the distances I wanted to walk, I needed something more—something that would stimulate my peroneal nerve, responsible for lifting your toes, with each step. I wanted my own nerves stimulated to work my existing musculature. We had a brief honeymoon until my hands gave out in June from arthritic pain, and I couldn't use a cane because I could no longer use my swollen hands.

[13]Not walking properly, upright etc. causes no end of problems. The ball of your femur doesn't sit correctly in its joint and your acetabulum (the cup of that hip joint) wears differently. It puts your sacrum out of whack. It causes pain. It's a pain in the butt. Using Google, I saw that sores associated with WalkAide usage had already been reported to the FDA. Great. I contacted the local orthotics guy who was helping me with Oscar. He advised using a gel to place on the electrodes to enhance conductivity with the thought that 1) my skin was sensitive, and 2) additional substance to buffer my skin and enhance conductivity would alleviate the problem. I tried this, but in short, it did not work.

me, I ignored it. Worse yet, I ignored it and then attempted to force it to bend to my will the way I had been taught. Control your environment, body, and others through your absolute determination. Through this experience, I realized that this theme kept coming up, and I was clearly not learning the lesson.

At about the same time, Adam and I shared some wild thought: we should try P90X, the extreme fitness program. We embraced what we believed to be a much healthier diet with lots of meat, vegetables, whey smoothies, and brown rice. It was great fun, and as an obsessive, I had to continually repeat the program which undoubtedly resulted in later health issues because of this specific diet I had adopted. I'm not saying the health issue of which I speak of never would have happened, but only that I surely accelerated its appearance with my new diet. Adam thrived with the P90X diet and fitness program, our genetics, obviously, greatly differ. I later learned that some of my food sensitivities coincide with foods recommended for P90X participants.

On June 18 2012, I woke up with a very sore right hand and wrist and a slightly sore left hand. I dutifully changed my laptop set-up to make it more ergonomic, began Aikido hand stretches with the advice of a friend, and otherwise tried to ignore what, to me, was painfully obvious,[14] pun intended. By June 29, Adam was driving me to all my appointments because I could

---

[14]There aren't many things biologically that cause symmetric pain or difficulty. My first guess was rheumatoid arthritis.

not use my hands. It was painful to pull up my pants after using the bathroom, hold a coffee cup, set the table (let alone cook), get up from a chair using my hands as leverage, use my cane, and, therefore, walk etc. You get the picture.

My physical therapist assured me that I was structurally stable and refused to listen to my concerns. I began informing my medical doctors of this new development. My neurologist assured me it was not of nervous system origin. My general practitioner, who didn't even bother to examine my hands, ordered an x-ray and referred me to a rheumatologist. From his nonchalant behavior and lack of professionalism, I knew it was the last time I would see him. Note to self: Find a new GP.

***

It was at this juncture, in the last days of July, that I received an email from a friend asking me to assess the scientific validity (also known as BS factor) of some work she was looking at. Could these ideas possibly help us? She had just been alerted to more immune issues of her own. We had a regular club going it seemed. What I read floored me. She had forwarded me information about Dr. Loren Cordain's talks regarding immune issues and the paleo diet.[15] Also forwarded was information about a researcher, Dr. Alessio Fasano, who does work on leaky gut.[16] I

---

[15]Dr. Loren Cordain, *The Paleo Diet*, 2001.
[16]Dr. Alessio Fasano, *Gluten Freedom*, 2013, and *Leaky Gut and Autoimmune Diseases*, Pub Med, 2012

sat and watched Cordain's talk, and it made so much sense to me. It wasn't just some new fad claiming to be a cure; it actually made scientific sense. They were speaking my language! I wrote down the citations on Cordain's slides and read them.

I was so convinced, I began paleo on August 1, 2012. I dove into reading Fasano's research of linking leaky gut syndrome with auto-immune disease. Between Cordain and Fasano, I believed I had my answer as to why I developed auto-immune issues.

***

That same day, I saw the physician's assistant (PA) in the rheumatology office. By this time, my hands were quite swollen, and the pain had reached my shoulders and neck as well. I just wanted a confirmation of my suspicions so that I could make necessary changes and get on with life. Adam's life had been totally turned upside down trying to run his two companies and a household while listening to me gasp with pain whenever I attempted to use my hands or shoulders. I was a wreck and utterly useless. I briefly considered keeping quiet about my new thoughts about my health, but you can't exactly "go paleo" without notice. I had to empty the house of all the non-paleo items like flour, pasta, legumes, and canned tomatoes. I needed help to accomplish this task. So, I told Adam I needed to go paleo and why; I just didn't tell him there might be another auto-immune issue at play. I explained the research to him, and he, being an engineer, did a lot of reading on the subject as well. He was very supportive of this new approach.

More tests, discoveries, office visits, and disappointments followed.

The physician's assistant was very pleasant. She examined my swollen hands, ordered tests, and confided to me that 1) she herself had rheumatoid arthritis and 2) she would no longer be working as the PA in that office. Great. My cyclic citrullinated peptide (CCP) antibody test came back negative, but the lab botched the Rheumatoid Factor (RF) test. I asked that the doctor (who the PA worked for) order additional tests since I had to be redrawn for the RF; I had just discovered that all women in my family have Hashimoto's (another auto-immune issue), and I wanted to check my thyroid function. He declined via his nurse, and I learned that he didn't realize I'd already seen his PA because he didn't bother to read my file. Scratch another MD.

By this time, I was in so much pain I was close to not being able to function. If I had to get up in the middle of the night to use the bathroom, I rolled out of bed but had trouble sitting on the toilet as that required my hands to sit safely. I couldn't get back into bed, so I slept on the floor with a blanket. Life was truly becoming depressing.

**

On August 14 I visited a different rheumatologist's office. I walked by rooms full of people sitting in hospital lounge chairs hooked up to intravenous drips. I silently swore that I was not doing that BS. The doctor examined my hands, my negative CCP and RF results, and diagnosed me with inflammatory polyarthritis which is a nice way of saying sero-negative rheumatoid arthritis. He was very young, very cocky, but knowledgeable—in traditional AMA-style medicine. Even with the negative results, his exact words were, "Looks like a duck, quacks like a duck—it's a duck." He wanted me on Methotrexate, the "gold standard" for RA treatment, immediately. He wanted me in one of those lounge chairs being infused with drugs. I said no. I was going to Japan in September and was not going to be on a new drug while out of the country. I knew my body well enough not to do that. This decision would prove to be monumental. It was the beginning of my questioning what I believed, questioning my scientific training and questioning the limits of the answers that science offers.

I told him that I planned on following the paleo diet and had, in fact, already started. He frowned and said, since he worked in Boulder, he'd seen it all. Diet was definitely not going to change my hands. The current scientific research showed that the faster you could get the swelling and pain under control, the better the long-term prognosis for the disease. Pain and swelling means that damage is ongoing. He encouraged me to at least begin oral prednisone. We could revisit the Methotrexate discussion when I returned from Japan. I declined and left the office. I got as far as the building lobby before my brain kicked in. How could I turn my back on scientific data that plainly showed that the faster I was able to get the damage under control, the better my prognosis? What fun is Japan going to be when I'm in so much pain?

I decided to start prednisone to ease the swelling and excruciating pain but to continue with the paleo diet. I retraced my steps to his office and asked them to call in the prednisone prescription, please. I really wanted to believe the diet would work, but I didn't yet trust in it fully. I only had anecdotal evidence from the web and tons of books on paleo. What if I chose the wrong path? Looking at this decision now, I see the similarity to the Betaseron decision. Old school had won that day. You could also say fear won that day. I was desperate. I was just diagnosed with more immune system issues.

I rarely saw doctors unless I had to. I didn't like their labels, their judgements, and the way they pretend to fully understand what is going on with you personally. With the misdiagnosis of multiple sclerosis back in 1991, I was forever tasked with trying to explain that mistrust. I finally gave up because it was just more stress for me, and the doc would always give me this eye roll like I just didn't want to admit something. So infuriating. Most physicians who saw me—and I did get tricky and start to see docs not in the same health-care system because my records are not shared across a network so I didn't have to hear "oh I see you have xyz..." all over again—treated me like a medical marvel of immune issues. All this to say, I had my guard up when I first saw the functional medicine physician, Dr. Jill, the very next day.

CHAPTER 29

Functional Medicine

Dr. Jill, an MD, who remains my main doctor and personal angel incarnate, was pleased to see I was already paleo and set out a plan to get me onto natural anti-inflammatories. She ordered testing to find out exactly what foods I was allergic to, and what specific genetic coding I carry which may cause nutritional deficiencies. I also filled out an extensive personal and medical history.

When the tests came back in mid-September, I was not amused.

I am host to a healthy population of Campylobacter bacteria (implicated in RA) and have fungal dysbiosis and small-intestinal bacterial overgrowth. I carry genes that are positive for celiac disease (DQ2) and I have a specific methylation mutation in my folate pathway that precludes me from taking many pharmaceuticals including Methotrexate—a folate antagonist.

Oh, and I harbor an unknown parasite. Clearly, I need to start charging rent.

Aside from the huge number of foods I knew I was allergic to (tree nuts, peanuts, shellfish, berries etc.), I am allergic to dairy, eggs, brown rice and a host of additional food items. I was now convinced the way I had been eating my entire life (particularly during P90X with whey protein and brown rice) was part of my entire immune system picture. Eating things that inflame your system is simply not good for you. I began taking a multitude of supplements based on my MD's expertise and the test findings. My body was depleted of a large number of nutrients. In order to get well, I needed to remedy that situation. Aside from that, I also needed to rid myself of the yeast and the bad bacteria. This was going to be quite the undertaking. Little did I know just how mighty a challenge this would turn out to be.

Dr. Jill and I share a love for data and science, the need to continue to heal our inner little girls, and the understanding of how much trauma can affect your total health picture. She admitted to me that she was concerned I would fire her, too. After all, I had fired several doctors before seeing her. Recently, I have come to depend on Jill even more to watch over my data and what she believes is needed as I quiet my analytical side, allow myself to feel more, live in the now, and pay attention to spirit instead of the numbers. More on that later.

We went to Japan as planned and returned in October. Being convinced as I was of the impact of my diet on my conditions, I wanted to postpone the discussion of Methotrexate. In the end, my rheumatologist agreed to extend the low-dose predni-sone until the end of December—no further. When I started tapering off the prednisone, I was terrified. I continued with my supplements, and Dr. Jill continued to modify them as she saw fit. I tried several different supplements in the quest to rid myself of yeast only to make myself very sick. Going back to the drawing board and attempting to return to some sense of stabil-ity seemed to be my normal state. It was terribly frustrating.

The end of December also saw the end of the low-dose predni-sone taper. I had stuck to the paleo diet with all of the addi-tional requirements for auto-immune disorders (no tomatoes, nightshades, etc.) since August 1. I was pain-free. It worked. All of the supplements and the very strict diet (call it paleo on ste-roids, ha, ha) worked. Yet I was still terrified. I felt like a fraud. I was concerned the steroids dampened the pain, but one might see damage inside my hands when one looked. I felt like I was hiding a secret and that the rheumatologist would look at my hands and tell me the destruction he saw, what I had allowed to occur; but I had no pain. I still believed more in science than what I actually saw, felt, or experienced, a theme that would recur for some time to come.

***

I saw the rheumatologist in January 2013. He took my hands in his and peered at them, poked and prodded. I couldn't even meet his eyes I was so afraid. He said, "What's your secret?" I responded, "Strict paleo and my functional medicine MD's supplements."

He asked if I wanted an ultrasound to look inside my hands to see if we could find any ongoing disease activity. We looked and found nothing. The ultrasound revealed nada, zip, no swelling, no internal inflammation. The arthritis was in remission or just plain gone. I prefer to think of it as the latter. I reversed a condition that he had described as incurable not even six months before on August 14th.[17]

---

[17] I no longer see traditional medicine professionals, and I see my functional medicine MD regularly. I additionally stopped injecting Betaseron with the blessing of that same doctor. Over the years I depended on others to help me inject where I could not reach in order to rotate sites, but the repeated and frequent injections had made a mess of my body. I came to understand the drug had wreaked havoc on my immune system, as well. I needed to heal both physically and emotionally.

CHAPTER 30

Japan, Part 2

Our careening taxi arrived at the hospital ER. Nobody spoke English which isn't surprising since we were in Japan—although we were specifically told to go to this particular hospital because someone who did speak English was supposed to be present to help us. Alas, what do you do?

I was dying. I thought of the promise I made the ER doctor at home: don't hesitate. My breath had become very shallow, and I could no longer feel my hands or arms; Adam was going to have to give me an injection with the EpiPen. I showed him where to administer the injection, and in front of an ER full of people enthralled with two gaijin (foreigners) in their midst, he stabbed me in the thigh, through my clothes, with the EpiPen. I could breathe. I'm not going to die in Japan. That was my exact thought. I felt incredible relief, but I had also been injected with epinephrine. I felt like an out-of-control locomotive.

The staff didn't even notice. One of the people in the waiting area of the ER led us over to a nurse's station where I, unceremoniously, dropped the used EpiPen onto her desk. This finally resulted in some scurrying about. They were not pleased that I had used an epi in their ER waiting room; I was in no mood for bullshit given I was high on a whopping dose of epinephrine. The five MDs gathered around my bed spoke little English. I spoke little Japanese as stated earlier. This was one rough conversation. Finally, I recalled I had Dr. Gunshin's paperwork in my purse. Holding it in my hand, I repeatedly pointed at it, shoved it at them, and pantomimed phoning. They went away with the paperwork and came back with different attitudes.

These very young MDs were very capable. The ER was just an open ward so I watched them administering to a traumatic brain injury in addition to the medical ailments of other patients. They just didn't know what to make of me until they spoke with Dr. Gunshin in Tokyo. I also was able to get the neurologist, the oldest of the group, to confirm the rash I had on my scalp, shoulders, and neck was indeed caused by BAM-BAMs. This was progress.

Well, obviously, I couldn't take BAM-BAMs anymore. Now what to do about trigeminal neuralgia? They decided on a different medication similar to what I was taking. I asked what dose they recommended while trying to tell them that I react very strongly to medication. This fell on deaf ears as they talked among themselves and consulted their cell phones. Great, we'll deal with that tomorrow, I thought. Someone would be by bright and early, 5AM, with a dose of the replacement med.

Keep in mind we had no internet access and no way to make an international phone call. I would've otherwise been on the phone with my MDs stateside, but there's a fifteen-hour time difference. I had no info with which to compare medications, probable mode of action, or even see to which drug class it belonged. I never take meds without researching them, but there's always a first time, right? I was not happy about this, but I didn't see a way around it. I'd do some research and make the necessary phone calls when I got back to the hotel.

Obviously, we had to stay the night in ICU. I was receiving an IV drip to calm my immune system and stop the allergic reaction. We took a bizarre late-night stroll through Kobe hospital, me in a wheelchair, hanging onto my IV stand, looking for any kind of phone or internet access so I might speak to my doctors in the US or do pharmacology research on the internet. We met some lovely people working at the hospital convenience store who had nothing I could eat but were helpful, cheerful, and sympathetic.

We both slept in the hospital bed. OK, Adam slept, and I listened to all of the noises. It reminded me of being a kid. I felt strangely comfortable in this environment; everything felt familiar, and it allowed me to not focus on anything unsettling about our current situation. It allowed me to stay out of my body and in my head which was where I preferred to be at that point in my life. The rhythmic beeping of the monitors, the man with the head injury moaning, a nurse singing to him to calm him, and coughing. Lots of coughing. I knew that I'd be lucky to get out of here without catching whatever virus everybody had. We'd had masks on the entire time, the curtains to our little ICU corner pulled, and I stole a bottle of hand sanitizer from the nurse's station on my way back from the restroom earlier in the evening.

It would be an understatement to say that I was very worried at this point, but I knew I needed to keep it under control. I didn't want to upset Adam further by letting him see how I really felt about this situation. It was enough that this was our second hospital visit of the vacation, and I knew there were more to come.

They didn't show up with the medication at 5:00 AM. When they did, they wanted me to take three capsules. My intuition was screaming at me to take only one. Adam quickly pocketed the other two. I was supposed to be released by 6:00 AM, but it took me threatening to pull my IV line out to finally get the MD to appear. They gave me more medication for the trip home to the States, reminded me to call Dr. Gunshin in Tokyo, and let me loose over four hours past when they had originally told me I could leave. It was the weekend, and their accounting office was not open. We eventually walked out without paying but with a promise to "be in touch." It was an amazingly surreal experience.

The sun was dazzling and immediately warmed my face as we stood there on the sidewalk, trying to get our bearings and locate the taxi queue. The air was clear and fresh. It stung my lungs after being cooped up in the warm hospital. I wasn't terribly familiar with this part of the city; but it struck me how absolutely beautiful the city of Kobe was. It literally glittered in the sun, and I was ever so grateful to be alive. Tears of joy filled my eyes. Recalling this story always brings me to tears. It was just that profound.

We grabbed a taxi back to the Kobe Crowne Plaza Hotel just in time to catch the breakfast brunch. It was now approaching eighteen hours since I'd consumed anything. We sat in the private lounge on the top floor of the hotel in somewhat of a stupor, looking at the best view in Kobe. They have magnificent coffee machines there which also exude magnificent cocoa. I told Adam to please keep the cocoa coming as we ate breakfast. No, I was not supposed to be drinking cocoa with its overabundance of sugar and dairy, but I had almost died the evening before. I can't print what I was thinking at that time, and how much I simply did not care. I understand that one of the worst things to do at that point was to consume things I know I'm allergic to (dairy) or are not good for me (sugar), with my gut undoubtedly compromised by the drugs and leaking allergens into my bloodstream, but I simply didn't care. Near-death experiences will do that to you.

I recall having a brief discussion about the large amount of paperwork that must be involved with the repatriation of bodies. Adam said that he would have called for backup. Things just had to be amusing at this point.

I checked email. There was a response to my rash photos from my neurologist in the US: stop taking the BAM-BAMs and possibly go to a hospital. Done and done. Damn, she's going to love this story, I thought.

There was also a response from my functional med MD, Jill, which I will insert here:

I just happened to come across today.... Carbamazepine in a folate antagonist. We know that you have issues with methylation based on testing that you are positive for one copy of abnormal C677T gene for MTHFR. For that reason you will have more trouble methylating and converting to active folate (about 60% of activity of a normal person). When patients are undermethylating, they will produce more histamine = rash, anaphylaxis, etc... This means that the Carbamazepine could potentially be a key in your increase in histamine reactions.

Translation: I carried genetic defects that make my allergic reactions worse than average, and BAM-BAMs exacerbated this.

I read this and laughed. Finally I was getting at the reasons I had been having problems all of my life.

***

Dr. Gunshin worked the evening ER shift, so we had plenty of time to kill before I could speak with him. We had to have all of our travel plans changed, so we started on that. We had planned to go to Matsue, which is very remote on the western side of the main island; that clearly was not happening now. I needed to be back in Tokyo with Dr. Gunshin—not someplace far away.

By the time we went downtown Kobe to kill more time—we wouldn't leave to go back to Tokyo until the next morning—

my face and throat were strangely numb. I sucked on cough drops to keep myself aware of my ability to swallow (or not) and kept quiet. My airway was uncompromised, and I could breathe. Adam didn't need to know that I was also allergic to the drug they gave me at the hospital to replace BAM-BAMs. I knew I couldn't take more and also realized that had I taken all three capsules, we'd be going back to the hospital at this point. What a charming thought. That 25mg capsule was the only one I took. The trigeminal neuralgia pain was inexplicably gone. I didn't know or understand why, but I was thrilled it had disappeared.

When I spoke to Dr. Gunshin that evening, he apologized for what we had experienced—as if it were somehow his fault. He categorically told us we could not go back home immediately— not that we wanted to— because I needed to be stable before getting on a plane. I was to come back to Tokyo immediately where he could monitor me. When was I coming back, and when could he see me? No problem. I will never complain about an extra week in Tokyo.

I was back in Tokyo the next day and had a lovely reunion with Dr. Gunshin shortly after. He gave me medication to take with me on the plane in case the neuralgia returned on our way home. I knew I wouldn't take it. Not that I didn't trust him; both he and the pharmacist had a pow-wow and decided this was the safest thing for me to take should I absolutely require it. I was just hesitant to take anything at this point--let alone while on an airplane over the Pacific Ocean.[18]

In retrospect, I realize how much I had to do with manifesting this situation. I had packed six EpiPens. Did I really think I was going to use six? Medically speaking, that's not terribly likely. What I was doing was living with the consciousness of fear. Deciding to take six showed how afraid I was of allergic reactions at that time. Energetically speaking, you attract what you project. Like attracts like, so fear attracts fear. In bringing six EpiPens, I was attracting the energy of this major mishap in some form or another.

All of the times I thought "this would make a great story" or "Jill will love this story" again just brings me the energy of fantastical and extraordinary events. It literally draws those experiences to you. I now am very careful what I think about as consciousness is everything. I envision a blissful and boring existence.

***

I now wonder who spoke to me and told me to take just one capsule and not the three that the doctors recommended. Was it Archangel Michael, Rafael, or Gabriel? Or was it a collective

---

[18]I saw my neurologist when I returned to the US. She told me I could no longer take any of the meds for trigeminal neuralgia—they were too closely related in their pharmacology. I had already come to the same conclusion when I was able to do my own research. We're all thrilled the trigeminal neuralgia pain went away, but nobody is more thrilled than I am.

shout? I don't know, but I do remember how strongly I was receiving that message. I remain so grateful for that guidance.

It was a time of miscommunication. We couldn't reach anyone on the outside or in the US, couldn't get to a working phone or computer, and didn't, for the most part, speak Japanese. So what navigation system was I using? My intuition. Despite all the education and studying that gave me the knowledge to understand the dense jargon in that email from Jill, I was now making decisions for my own well-being from intuition; it was a clear sign that I was headed home, physically, mentally, and spiritually.

PART FOUR

The Guiding Lights

CHAPTER 31

Forgiveness

I had a long journey of self-forgiveness ahead of me I had betrayed myself in so many ways. I acted and behaved aggressively and boy-like to get accolades from my father. I didn't listen to my body and tried to tune out my intuition because it wasn't hard science and, therefore, I felt might lead me astray. I basically had lost my ability to trust my inner compass; to listen as keenly as I remember doing when I was a child.[19]

I went through a period of taking many online courses in self-discovery and self-improvement. My introduction to energy work was in 2016 when I was taking a course on forgiveness. The woman teaching the course, Marcy, was a gifted energy worker, and I would take several classes with her. During this time, I realized forgiveness wasn't just about finding or writing letters to people (to be or not to be delivered). I needed to learn how to forgive myself for doing things, acting in a particular manner, or not paying attention to or caring for myself. This is a path of taking responsibility for what I had done and making amends with myself and others. I looked up many people I felt I owed an apology. It was cathartic and healing. I couldn't find everyone I wanted to, but I tried.

There is a woman who worked as a receptionist at a medical office who was surly, opinionated, and abrasive. I knew I needed to apologize to her but was unsure whether she would accept it.

---

[19]I started a blog, Incurablyrude.com in 2014 to share my experiences with disability, neurological issues, functional medicine and related topics. Several years later, I realized that not only did I not think of myself as incurable, but I did not like the label rude either. I didn't want to be rude and aggressive for approval from my father (be a boy), which is what I'd been doing all of my life. That was just not the authentic me. I took the blog down, I relinquished my wheelchair parking tag, and I refused to take any additional compensation from my disability policy. Believing in my healing just didn't allow for those other things in my life. In my opinion, you can't accept the trappings of a condition whether it be a parking tag or monetary compensation and at the same time hold the belief you are healing and well. Those bestowing the parking tag or money upon you label you with a condition and it is necessary to have that condition in order to receive and fully accept the benefits. For me, after all I'd been through in childhood, academia, and in many damaging relationships—including the one with myself—it was not possible to hold both beliefs at the same time. I knew which one I preferred.

We hadn't seen each other in years. She and I never got along, and one day while I was visiting, she managed to set me off. I was calm with an even voice, but my tone was deadly as I told her off, seemingly with such success that she began to cry and rushed off, disappearing into the back of the office. I felt, at that time, that I had bested her. I won. It couldn't have been further from the truth, of course. That negativity, that rudeness only brings the same back to you. It doesn't feel good. It causes harm within you that you may not see.

Several years later, I went back to that office and found her. I apologized for my behavior and asked for her understanding and forgiveness. She was accepting and more gracious than I deserved. She hugged me, and I felt renewed in some way I can't explain. I remember feeling that some little piece of me had come back home, and I wondered what its absence had costs me for those interim years.

As I continued this work, I realized how much more comfortable I felt, as if I had found the real me. I would recognize situations where I could see what my old self would have done and be thankful that I no longer felt that l that I needed to behave that way. I was free to choose my path. I didn't have to do things to please others or to illicit a certain reaction, and it felt so liberating.

CHAPTER 32

Growth

I have worked for many years to be able to forgive my mother for her part in contributing to the idea that there will always be something wrong with me. I am happy to report we now have a good relationship wherein I recognize that she, just like all the rest of us, was greatly influenced by her upbringing, beliefs, and genetics. I no longer blame either of my parents for anything. Forgiveness holds no room for blame. Only with forgiveness may I be free.

I ended up doing some additional personal healing with Marcy, the person who taught the class on forgiveness. During one of our sessions, I realized that she was "seeing" what I was. At one point I was in a dark, cavernous space, holding a torch or some light in my right hand, while speaking to a group of people who were gathered there with me; they were made of pure light— light beings, I named them. It was like the cave in Guam where

I wanted to be a part of that special little group of fish, feeling so secure and included. The moment was so magical that I quickly sketched the scene after the session ended. This was my first experience of being able to see energy.

This was all a revelation to me. I was a believer in the unseen now. It was the beginnings of understanding that my world of science, data, proof, and what I could see with my eyes was not the only thing out there and, quite possibly, not the answer to everything. Little did I know where this journey would all lead me.

CHAPTER 33

Trauma

Listening to a presentation on trauma by Nicki Gratrix in May 2017, I found myself talking back to the video as I multi-tasked cleaning and doing chores. I remember I agreed with a lot of the points she made with her presentation, and it made me think about how messed up my childhood was. The next morning, I could barely get out of bed my low back hurt so badly. In fact, I was quick to notice it felt exactly how it did when I had a bulging disc while working at the university. How interesting; I made the connection to the talks on trauma immediately.

Wow, did I really have a disc issue—as was elucidated by an MRI while at the university—or had it been trauma-related all along? I thought back to how the early uses of MRIs saw spots (abnormalities) come and go in the brains of asymptomatic people. Definitely more to ponder here, I thought.

I had spent most of my life trying to justify why being a military brat was an advantage: you could survive anywhere, adapt to any situation, change didn't bother you, you became used to seeing friends come and go, you lived with no attachments. What I realized was that this was actually a justification for dealing with something that I had no control over. When you're a military brat what you really end up experiencing is a broken household, at least one absent parent, lack of guidance, the need of the child to become more like a parent, the need of the child to become an adult before their time, constant turnover in friends and people close to you, possible substance abuse, lack of support and more. This is not a recipe for a healthy child physically or psychologically.

I found myself at the offices of Dr. Jane Ray, looking for help via acupuncture. I also looked to Liz Stewart, an experienced Rolfer, for additional help with my back issues. In June 2018, I found more answers in Nicole Sachs' 28-day challenge online and her book, *The Meaning of Truth*. Nicole was a patient of Dr. John Sarno. Sarno believed chronic pain (Tension Myositis Syndrome or TMS) is caused by repressed emotions. It was a real eye-opener when I started making my lists of traumas past and present such that I could begin journaling on them. I realized my lists of traumas were quite extensive and felt my back pain change for the better after journaling while following the 28-day challenge. Nicole had another practitioner, Caroline, working with her, and I jumped at an opportunity to sign up with Caroline. Thus began a relationship I cherish which is still ongoing. Caroline has been instrumental in my continued recovery and brought me from a place of cringing when the phone rang with the thought that it may be my mother to a place where I embrace Spirit and am finding peace. Caroline also introduced me to another two healers I rely upon, Josh and Maryann.

Dr. Ray soon referred me to a physical therapist with extraordinary talents as an energy worker, Lori. When I first started seeing Lori, I was often in a wheelchair and had trouble getting on the exam table. I've definitely had ups and downs, but my trajectory is decidedly moving in the right direction under her care and guidance. At first, I was very worried she was feeling what I was feeling because she exclaims as the energy is released and is moving. She assured me that she felt the intensity of the energy, but not the pain I was experiencing in the same way. What a relief that was!

When Caroline asked me if I had ever seen a medium, I was intrigued. No, but I was definitely interested if she thought we would gain insight. I looked over the list of names she sent for my perusal. I was drawn immediately to one link, clicked it to visit the website, and immediately knew this woman was important to me. I felt like I had always known her. That she was a long-lost friend. That's how my relationship with Maryann began in this lifetime. I know our relationship will not end. We've known each other in past lives, and I know our cosmic dance of friendship will endure all.

CHAPTER 34

Consciousness

While Maryann and I began as medium and client in this timeline, it quickly turned into a friendship where we shared thoughts, visions, information on energy healing, discussions of the different spiritual dimensions of reality, and the world of energy at large. Maryann taught me an enormous amount of useful information, and I continue to gain a wealth of knowledge from our discussions.

Working with this handful of energy workers was amazing, intense, and allowed me to see how I was operating in this world. I understood that I needed to change my beliefs and the way I interacted with the world in order to heal physically and emotionally. I saw that I operated in a very analytical, using-my-brain-only manner which contributed to my physical illness. As my consciousness expanded, and the more

I listened to my body and its natural abilities—using less drugs—the better I felt.

I began mentoring with Maryann. I learned about protecting myself energetically, disengaging from people who were sucking energy from me, and the beginnings of navigating life in a new way. As the work continued, we soon came to a point where I was asked whether I was sure that I wanted to continue to learn more and move forward on this path. Once you go past a certain point, you can't go back. You can't un-see or unlearn what you have experienced. It all sounded very *Matrix*-like to me— will you choose the Red Pill or the Blue Pill? It was exactly that and so much more. I believe I chose to move forward on the path of spirituality because of an inner calling, knowing there was something else besides just what I was seeing with my eyes. I had already seen the light beings in the session with Marcy.

Over time, my small circle of friends became even smaller. I didn't seem to have much in common with most people anymore. I wasn't interested in distractions of arguments, one-upmanship, conflict, or family drama. I began to see how meaningless and small those things were in relationship to the whole of being loving and joyful. Look at things in a new light, and you begin to have different experiences and see the world in an entirely different manner. The universe presents me with things for my learning and growth. Things happen for me; the universe works for me. This is a much lighter way to approach life rather than trying to mold and control it. Yes, at first you think you are crazy, then you find the tribe of people to whom you can relate.

CHAPTER 35

Protection

I began to see archangels, my guides, and even Jesus occasionally when working with Maryann. I ask the archangels to come to medical appointments with me for guidance and strength. One particular appointment found me having an allergic reaction to a numbing agent the doctor used. She stopped the procedure, but I told her to wait while I had a quick conversation.

I asked the archangels who were in the room if it was safe for me to proceed with the procedure. I turned toward their energy, eyes open, and asked my question in my mind. I literally got the thumbs up from my smiling angels; I had been given the go ahead. The procedure was successfully completed, and all ended well. I didn't share everything I was seeing with the doctor, only the decision that we could proceed. I'm sure the doctor didn't write that in her notes, or maybe she wrote her patient hallucinated.

When Adam entered the room, the doctor told him I saw things. Adam told her I saw things all the time; this was not news and definitely not a reaction to the medication I was allergic to. Sometimes I see figures, maybe discern expressions like a frown or smile, and sometimes I just feel the energy of that expression or Divine Being.

Archangel Michael is most often around me. Archangel Rafael is often in attendance as well. Archangel Gabriel sometimes comes now also. Maybe they were all always there, and I have become better at sensing and seeing them.

I also realized I had been reading people in the past during complicated, possibly dangerous situations, for purposes of physical safety. Heinrich, my adrenaline-junkie friend from the gym, often put himself in compromising situations with questionable people which meant I often ended up in that unfortunate mix as well. I would occasionally refuse to even enter a room or business where Heinrich was supposed to attend a meeting. I felt so uncomfortable about the environment or was receiving such negative energy from people in the environment, I knew it was unsafe. Heinrich always trusted me, and we would leave.

I also now understood that my years of waiting tables years earlier, I had actually been reading people and predicting their wants and needs. I didn't have to wait for a customer to raise their hand, call out, or otherwise signal they needed me. I just somehow knew.

One of my early sessions with Maryann was due to an accident. My hand slipped while leaning against a door jamb at home which caused an unfortunate meeting of my ribcage and the door jamb. The force knocked the wind out of me, bringing me to my knees. I asked for assistance with my injury and had a lengthy session with Maryann. The archangels Michael and Rafael came to assist by carefully wrapping each rib and soothing with scalar wave energy during the session with my medium. All energetically, of course, the ribs wrapped and bathed in powerful energy which hastened their healing. Using a scale of 1 to 10 (10 being most intense), my pain level was brought from a 12.5 to a 2 during that session. To make things even more extraordinary, I had no bruising. None.

Caroline, as I mentioned, has been instrumental in introducing me to the healers I see. I trust her implicitly, and if she thinks I might benefit from meeting someone, I am happy to entertain the idea. I believe I that am connected with the healers, or people in general, that I am meant to meet or work with. I have ongoing relationships with a number of specific healers, but I see them for different reasons depending on what issue I am addressing and where their expertise lies. There is value in seeing different spiritual counselors because each contributes something different and has their own set of powerful skills. I let my intuition guide me to what person I need to see. Often it's my medium, Maryann, who I seek out for questions addressing past trauma or in dealing with my pets. Josh, who works in Theta Healing, brings me enlightened conversations and guidance on a regular basis. I also see Caroline and Lori regularly. My functional medicine doctor, Jill, is a firm believer in spirituality and its role in our health and wellness, so my healers meld nicely—many of them even know each other.

CHAPTER 36

Back to The Origin

In the beginning of my work with Maryann on my traumatic past, it was necessary to integrate parts of myself held back by past trauma into my current self so that I could fully heal. In order to be a healthy adult, I needed to heal the little girl inside of me. The part of my subconscious who is a small child we named Little Girl (LG). Fortunately, she is quite vocal. This was amazingly helpful as we were dealing with trauma and integrating the past as the LG could ask questions and have things clarified. We allowed her to tell us her story, her memories, the trauma she recalled, and we encouraged her to ask questions. We were letting my inner LG know that there was now a responsible adult in the room, namely me, and that I would look after and care for her. I was the caring, present parent that she had always lacked.

The LG was not easily convinced. I awoke one day to a rash on my neck and chest. I did the posture I've done since I was a kid, standing in front of the bathroom mirror, lifting my shirt, and surveying the rash. I wasn't excited about it. It didn't itch, and I knew exactly what it was. The LG was testing me. Would I really listen to her and take care of her? I told Adam it was nothing to be concerned about, but we needed to go to the emergency room and prove that everything was okay. They couldn't find anything in the blood workup they did. Everything seemed normal. The female doctor asked if I had ideas, and I told her I had been doing a lot of trauma work recently. I was sure this was the cause of the rash. The ER doctor was incredibly kind and generally receptive to my explanation. She said all she could do was treat the symptoms and prescribed meds for itching in case it went in that direction.

Several days later, the rash started to itch, and I turned to my spiritual healer, Maryann. When we began working, she perceived the rash in detail as the Divine illuminated corresponding sensations while she was in my field. As I look back over my notes for those sessions, I see that we were dealing with my limbic system: flight, fight, freeze responses. There are lots of references to my LG reacting to the old trigger--namely everything is an emergency--to which she was accustomed. When trying to assimilate the new calm state, problems arose. Several days into the work, the rash thankfully disappeared along with the itchiness. Taking its place was a most intense, crushing pain in both my arms, shoulders, and hands which left me rocking in my chair to comfort myself and search for relief.

Maryann determined we needed to address three past lives and current points of origin of this particular issue. The cycle of neglect and abuse had gone on for many lifetimes, and I needed to confront the higher selves of my parents; I needed to go back to the origin. In this session was the first time I experienced the glory and divinity of Jesus.

I sat in session with Maryann over Zoom; I felt the energy of angelic beings around me as Maryann spoke with her guides. I suddenly felt them recede into the background a bit as my existence was suffused with love like I'd never known. The sudden presence of the most intense energy I have experienced inspired awe as I sat silent, eyes closed, slightly rocking in my chair, my scalp tingling. I knew this Divine energy was Jesus. My heart wanted to burst open it was so full. I felt an all-encompassing complete love. I was submerged in this powerful energy, feeling warm, cared for, accepted, and fully supported. I actually felt Jesus take my hands in his and salve them with love.

The crushing pain flowed down my arms, and I felt it drip like water from my fingertips. Jesus told me that my hands which were searching for love need search no longer. Remembering this still brings tears to my eyes.

Maryann and I just sat quietly staring at each other over Zoom when she closed the session. She asked if I had "felt" that; I nodded in awe. There were no words to describe what had just happened. My pain was gone.

I had an appointment the very next day, and it was surreal.

Everything around me seemed like something I'd never seen before. It had snowed lightly overnight. It was like the world was a cake that had been lightly covered in powdered sugar. Everything just was extraordinarily beautiful. I spoke to people from this blissful fog. Somehow, I had changed. This was easily one of my most sacred experiences.

As we continued integrating my subconscious past into my present, LG came forward with enthusiasm. Now she had confidence about the future because she sees that I, the adult, have changed. LG was not pushed to run through doors as she was in the past as that little girl with no voice, but now asked what she wants. Before, she didn't bother voicing because she never would have received what she asked for, but she's now realizing that she's the governing voice. Through our sessions, I continued to perceive LG's voice and her questions while Maryann continued to clarify LG's voice and was the main go-between in conversations.

As the conversations continued between me, Maryann, and the LG, we realized that there were patterns and similarities between memories arising from different times and places. For instance, bullying at school and being bullied by Frank are similar and elicited similar unwanted manifestations. While the details of the memories differed, the traumas of the incidents and the resulting physical manifestations for me as an adult were the same. We came to think of this collection of memories as a library or a catalog of sorts. We called it The Memories of Wisdom™. In this catalog of the subconscious is stored all the things that had transpired, had been gone over and integrated by the LG—her memories of trauma. There was no need to continue playing the same experiences over again resulting in the same associated trauma and manifestations. The Memories of Wisdom™ continued to grow, and the most-gifted medium, Maryann, and I would point out when something was just another flavor of something already gone over, dealt with, catalogued, and stored. No need to react to that. It is not new to you LG.

Jesus again joined a session to help (Maryann, The Divine, me, and the LG) when the LG was having tremendous doubt and misgivings. Again, the presence of all-consuming love filled the room, filled my body and soul, my scalp tingled, and He spoke to the LG to assuage her trepidation: "Do you remember I told you I loved you? I'm wiping away doubt. You are loved, worthy, and deserved. If I show up, nobody else matters."

I felt infused with these words; I hear them in my mind's eye with calmness and assuredness. Through this process, the LG grew up and became the Young Lady. We continued on until we caught up with my present self, having integrated all of my subconscious which had been held back by trauma.

CHAPTER 37

Awe

Our brown tabby, Edwin, is an extraordinary cat. Even though he left this mortal coil some time ago, I use the present tense when I talk about him because he has never really left. I had a great deal of guilt when Edwin passed away. Although I realized it wasn't my fault, somewhere I was thinking my intellect would get us out of the situation.

Pure hubris. At a young age, Edwin underwent a dramatic surgery because of a failing excretory (kidney) system. The commanding alpha cat of the household, he was too young and far too full of life and tenacity to leave us so soon. With the surgery we gambled on more life for our young rock star of a tabby; Edwin recovered successfully and was again our super tabby who supervised everything and everyone. After less than two years of post-surgical check-ups we had finally received the "everything is great" report from the veterinary hospital.

Within a month, things were anything but great. The night we said our final goodbyes in this dimension, the sunset was one of the most stunning I'd ever seen. I was so upset, not being in the same place spiritually as I am now, I drew the front drapes and couldn't look at the repeated amazing sunsets that paraded across the skies.

I was meditating a lot during that period of time, and Edwin came to me to ask who I thought was responsible for those skies awash in color. Edwin is a character, so I thought it was a bit cheeky, but I know now Jesus had a hand in it as well. It was only when I realized that Edwin was responsible for those skies--those messages--that I began to look anew at the setting sun. I knew now that I could hear messages, and feel Edwin; I knew, therefore, it was possible to receive these messages. I did not need to see it with my eyes here in our 3D world in order to believe it or for it to be true. I could feel this.

We have many pictures of Edwin overseeing Adam doing household tasks like dishwasher repair, plumbing, and toilets. He was curious about everything and watched intently peering into the toilet tank and crawling into the dishwasher. I found out later while working with Maryann, dealing with my intense grief and guilt over Edwin, that all of this learning served him well as this life was his last before he became a mentor cat spirit, teaching other felines the intricacies of being companions to their humans. His time here was over. He had evolved. One of Maryann's many unusual talents is that she can communicate with animals directly, both living and dead. Edwin showed her a globe covered with lights, each representing one of the cats he was mentoring. He still talks with me. I get reminders to look under the dishwasher where there used to be a leak. Now we find cat toys that one of our other felines, Vinny, our young orange tabby, has inexplicably been able to slide under the front cover of the dishwasher.

I can feel Edwin's energy in the house at times; I was further convinced of this when I would watch our other cats respond to the energy in the room and run around playfully as if another, unseen, cat was present. One morning, I was awake in bed watching our grey tabby, Garrus, run about excitedly. The next thing I knew Edwin, who had crossed over years ago, chased him out of the room.

Change the patterns in the quantum field of energy, and you can change matter. It's not the matter that emits the field. It's the field that creates matter. Change the pattern in the field, and the hologram changes. This is the belief of many people. Oh my, Edwin learned the trick to make a hologram of himself. He understands the unified field of energy which connects everything regardless of space and time.

When other beloved kitties pass on, he is quick to teach them about the spirit realm and how to communicate with us. Garrus was our long-legged, always ready-to-play, grey tabby. He was Edwin's playmate, but he longed to be the alpha of the house. The night Garrus left us, there was an amazing cloud shaped like his profile complete with long face and pointy nose which floated slowly across our view. Adam saw it and quickly pointed it out to me.

Zed, our large orange resident tabby was our main caretaker.

Zed was the oldest in the house, but only Garrus saw Zed as the alpha (boys will be boys). Zed was just a huge teddy bear who didn't care about anything except being snuggled and caring for us. He was so empathic; he always knew which one of us needed his warm, comforting presence and would just park on whomever needed his love the most. He always worried who would take care of us when his time came, and we assured him, energetically, that he would still be able to care for us—just a bit differently. Sitting with him and waiting for the drugs to take their final effect in his last moments, he would not leave. The vet actually went to her car to make phone calls and cancel appointments as things were not progressing as usual. I told Adam that, he too, needed to let Zed know that it was okay to go now. Edwin was waiting for him, and we would always be here. He could visit any time and continue to care for us.

Zed finally let go of his tether to join Edwin, but he is always here with me. I feel him on my lap, and I feel his comforting energy when I most crave it. I know that I will continue to feel his warmth and presence when I most need his comforting. I did not have the same guilt or sadness I had when Edwin crossed over when Zed moved onto Spirit because he's still here. I feel him.

CHAPTER 38

Truth-Telling

I took a wonderful wellness workshop from Caroline, my transformational coach and Intuitive Healer. I learned many incredibly useful tools and techniques for healing. In part of the workshop, we worked in smaller "family" groups to get to know each other and support one another through the process. The group I was in didn't seem much into actually getting together. We were all from very different places internally; it was difficult to find common ground let alone a time convenient for everyone to meet. At one point I mentioned believing in past or concurrent lives and was met with total silence and a bit of disdain. After that, I didn't feel particularly safe or heard.

I was taking a homeopathic remedy at this time which was bringing up all sorts of old trauma to release. Homeopathy works through bringing everything from symptoms to emotions up and out of the body instead of just shutting off or ameliorating symptoms to relieve them. It is common while treating one issue to have others come up and move out of the body, as well. I had a vision of being burned at the stake as a witch or healer in a previous life. Tied to the stake, the fire already lit, I peered through the rising smoke at the faces in the crowd who had come to enjoy the spectacle. I recognized two of the women from my family group who had dismissed my speaking of past-life experiences. They were near the back of the crowd watching with great interest. After that, I didn't attend any additional family group gatherings.

I have come to accept that I see and experience things that may seem odd or not possible to others. In the beginning, I was fearful of voicing what I was experiencing for fear of being ostracized or thought crazy. I now know that part of my journey is to own what I see and experience and to share it with others so it might inspire others to awaken and find their own voices and acknowledge their own experiences and visions. I was brutalized and silenced in past lifetimes for my convictions. This is a different era, and many of us are awakening. I've evolved to say, "You can't hurt me." Nobody's judgment can touch me. I speak my truth. Truth is accepting our divinity.

CHAPTER 39

Self-Worth

I was at the end of a Zoom meeting with Caroline discussing whether I would be attending her next healing workshop when my guide Dale first appeared. I have guides that help me with certain aspects of my life: companion animals, maintenance, and healing. Caroline was explaining the workshop and while I told her I would consider attending, I was also having an inner dialogue about my self-worth. Was it worth the money to attend the workshop? It was the kind of stuff many of us have going on inside of us if we pay attention.

I had no more thought that specific thought when a woosh of energy went by between me and my computer screen. I whipped my head to the left to follow the energy, asking Caroline if she had seen it. She had. Well, I said, I guess I better meditate and get to know that energy and what it's about. I confessed my feelings of low self-worth to Caroline which manifested that energy. Caroline and I closed our meeting, and I meditated. A new energy appeared to me in my meditation and introduced himself as Dale. My new guide who had suddenly appeared to tell me I was, indeed, worth the cost of the class. "Take the workshop," Dale told me, and I did.

CHAPTER 40

Manifesting

The carpeting in our home had been in much need of replacement for years: seams were apparent, carpet tacks were catching my socks. Then the COVID pandemic took hold. I was not even remotely interested in having workers or anyone in our home.

One night I dreamed that we collected throw rugs and carpet remnants and randomly taped them into place. The scraps didn't fit properly and were mismatched, but the carpet was new, clean, and we did it ourselves without having anyone come into our home.

Over the holidays we had a water leak in the dining room, and we slashed out a piece of water-logged carpet and padding in order to dry and treat the plywood underneath. When it came time to decide what to do about replacing the carpet in the dining room, I found myself on a hardware store site looking for room-sized pieces of carpet and was presented with an option of carpet tiles.

The tiles came in different sized squares, but the two-foot squares came in boxes with many different patterns in each box. We purchased enough to do the small dining room and continued on to do the entire main floor of the house. My dream had come to fruition.

CHAPTER 41

Discernment

My parents moved when they were eighty-four years old. My mother, severely vision-impaired due to macular degeneration, did not want to move. Always looking for greener grass somewhere else, my father was adamant. I was working at my computer soon after they supposedly got to their new location, and I realized my mother was in my living room with me, behind me as I worked. I turned to look at her. Her energy so apparent I outlined with my hands where she was to Adam as I said, "I don't know what has happened, but it isn't good. Someone is going to have to call and tell me because I am not spending time discerning what has transpired."

That evening my father called to tell me my mother had fallen, broken her hip, and was transferred via ambulance to a hospital 170 miles away from their new house. She had hip replacement surgery the following day.

CHAPTER 42

Companions to Guide Her Home

In her later years, our beloved princess cat, Madeline, dealt with irritable bowel syndrome and possibly more unknown issues which we felt unnecessary to test or biopsy for, given it would not have changed the care she received. She spent her days playing less and sleeping more, trying to find a comfortable resting position. At this point, we made the decision was made to speed her along her way back to the Divine Light. We have an at-home vet who happened to be out of town, but fortunately she supplied us with someone just as compassionate and loving as she is. The sedative was given, and Adam and I stroked Madeline while thanking her for her love and companionship.

After Madeline's second injection, I looked up as the vet

checked for a heartbeat with her stethoscope. As the tears streamed down my face, I saw our living room was full of cats. Maddy was walking away from me, her little swishy furry butt full of verve, while her brother Edwin awaited her. Behind him was Zed, Garrus, and Widge, all previous companions of ours who also had lived with Madeline. They all lined up in a row like the staged photo you see on the front of a bag of cat food. I was poking Adam in the back to tell him what I was seeing, and Madeline turned to look at me, at us leaning over her-now lifeless body, as if to say, "You're not coming?" It broke my heart. I wanted to jump in front of her and say, "Don't go!" but Edwin explained to her that she was crossing. We wouldn't be coming at this time.

CHAPTER 43

Dream Communication

During the COVID-19 pandemic there was much uproar over vaccines, masks, and isolation. My eldest brother took to tapping on my field at night. When someone close to me is thinking strongly about me, maybe because they have questions or concerns, they will create enough energy that I can feel it physically. Sometimes that means I feel them in the room with me, or I wake up thinking of them, awoken by that energy. It's like feeling someone is near you physically when their body is absent, but their energy is present.

With Ted during this time, I would have dreams of him asking me questions that I could not accurately perceive. I would sit on the edge of the bed, knowing it was Ted, and knowing he had questions about vaccinations. Perhaps he wondered which one to get or whether he should be vaccinated at all? I couldn't tell; energetically all I received was chatter.

This happened several nights in a row, and I finally just implored him, in my mind, to pick up the phone and call me such that he could ask the questions he wanted to ask of me. Basically, I sent energy back at him assuring him it was okay to ask. He phoned within several days, and we had a discussion about COVID and vaccines.

CHAPTER 44

Beauty

I had an adverse reaction to the COVID vaccination I received. I'm a scientist, and I believe in vaccines; I chose to receive the vaccine willingly. I expected things would go well and didn't think there would be an issue particularly since I received the most basic of the vaccines available.

All that said, I experienced neuralgia in the left side of my face and head, mostly affecting the facial, vestibular-cochlear, and trigeminal nerves. Because of my sensitivities to medications that specifically can help that type of pain (remember BAM BAMs?), I opted for alternating Tylenol and ibuprofen every three to four hours, for months, to deal with the pain. I received tiny amounts of relief by putting hot compresses on my face. I would stand at the sink with a washcloth under the hot water and sob not knowing what to do or where to turn.[20]

Things felt so dire I contemplated suicide every couple of days. However, my love for Adam, belief in the Divine and that I was meant to learn from the experience kept me from following through.

One day, as I was making my way from my desk to the bath-room sink to make a hot compress, I glanced out the window. The most amazing colorful sky greeted me. I knew I had to take a photo, no matter my pain, and searched for my iPod. I stood at the window succumbing to the glory of that colored sky, knowing that Jesus had a hand in it—maybe Edwin, too. Tears of pain flowing down my face, I basked in the utter glory of all of that beauty. I changed my nature of just going to the bath-room to deal with my pain, and I instead chose to see what The Divine had presented me with—that sky. The pain in my face melted away from a monumental 16 on my scale of 1 to 10 (10 being the worst) to a 7. I felt so grateful. Thank you, Jesus.

---

[20]My homeopathists, Marnie and Johanna, were the only humans who were able to effect change in my reaction to the COVID vaccine.

CHAPTER 45

Guidance

I've had migraines for many years which were finally ameliorated by my homeopathist. I still get them occasionally from lack of sleep or stress, but they are now easily dealt with by the wonders of modern pharmaceuticals. At one point in my healing journey, I developed a migraine that meds couldn't touch, and Dr. Jill prescribed a different med which typically works but leaves me with insomnia. This time, however, it didn't work on my headache either. I was just trying to cope. As I was setting the table for dinner, I pondered this dilemma, "Why should I bother trying the new med again when it didn't work before?" At that moment, I received an answer from Archangel Rafael, "Take the med now." His voice was so clear to me, it was as if he were speaking to me from across the room. Did I "hear" it or was the message sent energetically? I don't know, but I asked Adam to grab me a pill while I finished setting the table. I took the med, and this time it worked. My headache was gone.

CHAPTER 46

Assistance

Whenever I go to an appointment, I feel like a divine entourage comes with me. In fact, it is true. In the midst of the adverse vaccine reaction, I made many visits to the nearest Urgent Care where I found superb support from Steve and Steve who were the senior nurse practitioner (NP) and nurse on staff at that time. I had continual ear infections and things were resolving until I went in one day and my normal caretakers weren't there. The woman NP who I ended up seeing was not at all helpful and questioned everything I said in spite of the fact I had been visiting consistently for at least three weeks and there were copious records.

As usual, Archangel Michael was in attendance watching the proceedings. The woman NP said she needed to leave to clarify something, and Archangel Michael actually frowned and followed her out. I told Adam I just wanted to leave without getting any help, but that Michael had frowned. She had erred. She reentered the exam room with Michael trailing behind her. She was a completely different person. It was as if our previous conversation never happened. She was helpful, wrote me scrips for what I needed, was gracious, kind, and did not have any further bizarre or unrelated questions. We all left. Adam made quips about not pissing off archangels. Thank you, Michael, for your intervention on my behalf.

CHAPTER 47

Meditations

Traveling to Japan as often as we did, basically every six months, we were blessed to become acquainted with the Ginza Monk, Hideo. He was a Buddhist monk who was most often found silently standing at the busiest intersection of Ginza in Tokyo, in front of the Wako Building, with his bowl ready to accept alms from pedestrians who hurried by. He would give blessings in exchange for a donation. We always went to visit him the first day we were back in Tokyo. He was an absolute joy to behold, beamed love, and smelled of incense. When the COVID-19 pandemic hit, and we couldn't return to Japan, I incorporated the walk to Ginza to see him in my meditations.

The first year of the pandemic went by, 2020, and soon it became even easier to meet with Hideo in my meditations. In fact, he was no longer standing on his street corner but floating a bit above it. I immediately noticed the difference, and I wondered what it might mean. I googled "Ginza Monk" and found that he had succumbed to COVID on February 18, 2021. Maybe that explained why it became even easier to hold hands with him during my meditations as we did so many times on his street corner in Tokyo when we visited.

CHAPTER 48

Clarity

The last time we visited Japan was in November of 2022. It had been since fall of 2019 since we had returned due to the COVID-19 pandemic. We were in Kyoto and met up with an old friend thinking we were just going for coffee, but she had other plans. She wanted to spend the day sightseeing in Kyoto.

We have been to Kyoto many times and have been told by our many Japanese friends that we have visited more sites than most native Japanese. I think this is mostly true for us all in that we tend not to visit the spectacular in our own backyards while looking afar for the break from the norm. She suggested Sanjusangendo which happens to be my favorite place in Japan, but Adam and I were unsure because this really hadn't been the plan at all. As we stood and spoke with our friend, clad in her special kimono she had worn just for us, I suddenly thought,

"Yes, let's walk down to Sanjusangendo." Adam and I have visited this particular temple on many occasions; she had never seen it. This would be quite a treat.

The Buddhist temple was founded in 1164 and has a 120-meter-long main hall dating from 1266. Behind the hall is an amazing garden complete with a pond and koi. The inside of the hall is simply spectacular as it houses the main deity of the temple, the Thousand Armed Kannon. Also present are one thousand life-size statues of the Thousand Armed Kannon, mostly made in the 13th century, which stand on both the right and left sides of the main statue in two sets of 10 rows and 50 columns. The statues are made of Japanese cypress clad in gold leaf. In the very front row of the thousand Kannon statues and the main statue are 28 statues of guardian deities. There are also two famous statues of Fūjin, (first corner as you enter) and Raijin (last corner as you leave) at the corners of the entire display of statues. No photography is allowed, the air is incense-filled, and most of the time quiet murmuring from the crowd can be heard as they file past the stunning display, stopping occasionally to read the signs describing the guardian deities. Near the main statue, monks sell incense, candles and similar items while also stamping temple books; a monk is often chanting and rhythmically beating a chime and offering prayers to the main deity. It is a difficult place to leave, it is so enchanting. We would find ourselves just standing and watching the priests pray and chant while noticing the piles of gifts left for the deity which include huge bottles of sake and bowls of fruit and flowers. Some people are busy talking and zip through the carpeted hall in their stockinged feed on the outside of the slower lane while others linger and leave coins at every guardian deity.

It is said that if you look hard enough at the life-size Kannon, you will find yourself. Careful observers will note slight differences in the statues while others think they are identical. The original temple had nightingale floors which make a chirping sound when walked upon. These floors were used in the hallways of some temples and palaces to alert occupants of possible intruders. On our first visit we were lucky enough to experience the original floors. After years of many visitors, they eventually covered the flooring to protect the wood from the heavy traffic.

I sat in a temple wheelchair deemed clean enough for inside use as we like to proceed slowly, and I tire while walking back and forth along the 120-meter hall and the adjoining corridors. We continued slowly with the thought our friend had never seen this temple and the fact we never tire of visiting this most special location. We passed the first set of life-sized statues, the main deity, and now were along the second set of life-size statues as we read the signage for the guardian deities. As we neared the end, I could see there was a new sign in front of my favorite guardian deity, the Thunder God, Raijin. His eyes glowed with intensity as usual. Adam stopped as he knows I love the Raijin statue. The sign said to better feel Raijin's intense stare, kneel on the floor before him. I so wanted to do this, but there were several issues. Being in a chair, I had my shoes on. I needed to take my shoes off in order to step onto the carpeted floor. Could I lean over, remove my shoes, stow them behind me, exit the chair to kneel before Raijin, in a crowd without causing a commotion?[21] While I was contemplating this dilemma as I stared at Raijin, the statue spoke to me. "I see you," Raijin said. I timidly looked around like a kid caught whispering during class to see if anyone else heard.

Raijin continued, "Your life has been smoky. Most murky at times. Hang on, your time approaches. It will clear soon." I just stared at the statue and quietly thanked him for his message of acknowledgement and encouragement. Adam asked me what happened; I answered I'd explain when we were out of the flow of traffic.

As we rounded the corner on the other side of the statue display, a woman ran up to me excitedly. "You heard him." she said. "He spoke to you, and you heard him." I nodded. Her eyes were bright with intensity and belief. She knew herself to be right. The woman then repeated what Raijin had said to me. I held her hands and nodded while thanking her for coming forward. She caught up with her friends, occasionally turning and looking at me.

Our friend asked what this was all about, and I hesitated briefly before owning what had happened. "Sometimes I hear spirits,"

---

[21]The Japanese have a most strange relationship with disability. For instance, they will proclaim a path wheelchair-friendly only to put stairs in the middle. We once had the police called on us when I used a set of stairs while Adam carried my chair.

I said. Our friend was totally unsurprised as the Japanese speak to the gods (kami) all the time. One of the principles of Japan's native religion, Shinto, is that kami inhabit all things including forces of nature and landscape features.

When we returned home, I found and purchased a lovely print of Raijin which now hangs above my desk watching over me.

CHAPTER 49

Acceptance

In the spring of 2024 Adam and I drove up to my folks' new home in Montana for a visit. I was excited to see them because we had not been able to visit since prior to the COVID pandemic.

I was warned by friends that it may be difficult to see the changes in them given their obvious aging, but I disregarded that because I, too, had been getting older and grayer. Maybe we'd both be a bit surprised, but I was not concerned. I set the intention for the visit to have a lovely reunion with great conversation and food. I thought only positive thoughts about the visit.

The reunion went off without a hitch. Sure, my father wanted to make sure my mother would be cared for if something happened to him, so there was a certain amount of conversation about life, death, and statistics. After all, his need to control everything around him remains firmly intact. My mother seemed to mostly live in the now which was wonderful to see. No predicting the future or living in past with possible regrets or mistakes. Just right now. After this visit, I viewed them differently. I saw us all as the flawed and evolving beings that we are just trying to do the best we can with what we understand and perceive.

Sitting with my parents, I realized that I no longer was searching for their approval because I accept myself for who I am. I am grateful to myself for the awareness of my own evolution and that of the relationship with my parents, particularly my father. My father, my eternal hero, accepted me just as I am, as did my mother.

I was once a girl who wanted to be sent to her father half-way across the world in a suitcase like a box of cookies. I did everything I could to fit into a metaphorical box, to be "good enough."

The long way home is over. Now, that I love and accept myself, I feel profoundly loved.

PART FIVE

Homecoming

I was still very young when I became disillusioned with organized religion or with what we equate with spirit (but isn't). This resulted in me actively turning away from anything remotely resembling God or Spirit. Additionally, being a scientist requires you to seek proof, and often, the proof one is seeking does not conform to what we are taught to believe is possible.

That is a huge dichotomy. If you believe outright, something is not possible, can or will it occur? Is it likely to occur at all?

When I had to give up on what I believed to be true with traditional medical interventions and trust in functional medicine, it planted a seed. Maybe I didn't know everything I needed to? Maybe there are things yet to be discovered.

I don't mean to sound like I thought I knew everything there is to know, far from it. However, there is a huge gap between traditional medicine, which addresses things by silencing symptoms with drugs, and functional medicine, which addresses root causes to alleviate the symptoms. When I had to put my faith in something (functional medicine) I did not know and was unfamiliar with, it set my mind up for the freedom it now has. It opened my mind to possibility.

When I experienced something, whether heard, seen, or felt, I no longer jumped to the conclusion it wasn't possible. I was open to greater possibilities. I found that the more open to that possibility I became, the more I noticed the uncommon occurrence.

We all have the spark of The Creator in us; we are closest to The Creator when we create, whether that be cooking, planting, or writing. I know this to be true. I may have been disillusioned at a young age and turned away because of how far away "religion" is to Spirit, but The Creator/Spirit has always been with me and in me. I am eternally grateful.

Afterword

Jesus Told Me to Write

A handful of healers I have worked with tell me they saw me writing a book. Being able to write scientific papers and publishing in scientific journals is very different from the kind of writing I knew they were speaking of. I was never interested in writing anything but science. I often told Adam about the latest person who told me they saw me writing, and then I would dismiss it. While I always welcome the visions and thoughts of others, it was just not something I saw myself doing. That all changed in April of 2023 when I heard Jesus tell me that I had a story to tell to honor my path and to uplift others. I heard it clearly, and I started to type, this text pouring out of me.

I write this as a tribute to my soul and all it has experienced and endured. I write this as a tribute to The Divine who patiently waited for me to see and understand that what matters is love and joy. I understand those things in my childhood may have shaped who I became, but I don't want that to be my story. I feel that I am becoming so much more than the sum of those early experiences and traumas. I now understand that my fact-based upbringing and vocations did not hold the answers I sought. I can't say that I still seek the "answers" because now I just allow them instead of seeking them. The Divine has a much better plan than anything we could imagine or conceive, so it is best to follow your intuition and allow for the beauty and wonder to unfold before you.

Acknowledgements

I want to express my gratitude to the following people for their spiritual and physical guidance, and the ever-evolving conversations we've had: Caroline, Jane, Dr. Jill, the girl who talks to trees, Johanna, Josh, Liz, Lori, Marcy, Marnie, Maryann, and Tara. I also appreciate Josh for his perspective as an author and a friend.

I am thankful for the companionship of those who have walked alongside me on my journey: Alex, Bill, Cricket, Edwin, Freddie, Garrus, Jeremiah Wayne, Madeline, Mario, Max, Nikki, Nip, Priscilla, Samantha, Tali, Tasha, Tigger, Vinny, Widget, Wilma the Wild Thing, Xena, and Zed.

I am grateful to April for her expertise and support in bringing this book to fruition, to Rumi for her guidance and for massaging and polishing the manuscript, and to Wendy for her attention to manuscript detailing.

I thank Adam for assisting with the finishing touches and copy editing.

Finally, I wish to acknowledge The Creator, Jesus, Archangel Michael, Archangel Raphael, Archangel Gabriel, and my guides Kim, Carl, Elizabeth, Paul, Libby, Dale, and Carol for their guidance and always being with me.